The Architecture
of Failure

The Architecture of Failure

Douglas Murphy

Winchester, UK
Washington, USA

First published by Zero Books, 2012
Zero Books is an imprint of John Hunt Publishing Ltd., Laurel House, Station Approach,
Alresford, Hants, SO24 9JH, UK
office1@o-books.net
www.o-books.com

For distributor details and how to order please visit the 'Ordering' section on our website.

Text copyright: Douglas Murphy 2010

ISBN: 978 1 78099 022 4

A CIP catalogue record for this book is available from the British Library.

Design: Stuart Davies

Printed in the UK by CPI Antony Rowe
Printed in the USA by Offset Paperback Mfrs, Inc

We operate a distinctive and ethical publishing philosophy in all
areas of our business, from our global network of authors to
production and worldwide distribution.

CONTENTS

Was aufgetürmt gen Himmel steht,
Und auch der Mensch, so hold vertraut
Mit all der Schönheit, die er schaut,
Entschwindet und vergeht.

Matthäus von Collin, 'Wehmut'

Introduction

It is a pernicious cliché that architecture is the most optimistic of cultural activities, but like all clichés it is not lacking in truth. It takes a massive commitment to build something, an investment in the future that requires hope and more than a little faith that one's effort is worthwhile. Architecture is a symbol of growth, of longevity and of immortality. Architecture is monuments and memorials; it gives those who build a foothold in the future. Poets, brooders and melancholics do not build; they ponder, staring at fragments. The Saturnine disposition is not one that is suited to the erection of edifices.

But architecture is also the medium of the ruin. Architecture collapses, erodes and decays. It is overwhelmed by nature and the names inscribed into its surfaces become worn away until they are illegible. It is a symbol of the transience of all things. The ruin is the melancholic counterpart to the heavenward reaching of architecture, but at the same time this is often a comforting melancholy, a pleasantly sublime disappearance. We visit ruins rather than living in them, we stabilise our ruins to stop them from decaying too much; they become monuments in themselves.

We are, at the current time, experiencing a new period of *ruinenlust*. But the subject of this passion for ruins is modernism; many of the 20th century's experiments in changing the patterns of politics, aesthetics and life still exist; ever more poignant due to the faded urgency of their expressions of tomorrow. The ruins of modernism are the subject of an ever increasing amount of art and literature, figuring heavily in the work of contemporary artists such as Jane and Louise Wilson, Cyprien Galliard, Tacita Dean, or Jeremy Millar. Shot through with a melancholy which is more antagonistic than that of say, Caspar David Friedrich, the ruins of modernism are fragments of the drive towards a better world that did not come to pass. As opposed to the romantic ruin, which was a mapping of the future of our present through the figure of the past *(what you are we once were, what we are you soon will be)*, the modern ruin is the discovery of a lack in the present - a lack corresponding to a potential future that only existed in the past.

In one way this book is a contribution to this literature. But unlike most current ruin culture, which takes as its subject the monumental concrete architecture of the social democratic period after World War II, the subjects of this work are the earliest examples of capitalist modernity in architecture: the exhibition palaces of the late 19th century. Much loved but also much misunderstood, these behemoths of iron & glass are forerunners of nearly all the experiments that would come later in the name of modernism. Built in a rush of optimism, we will see that they were mostly pathetic failures. Designed by the most stringently rational minds, they were also confusing, contradictory, obscure and fragmented spaces. They presented compelling images of a better future but also the ruthless harshness of modernity; they were massive buildings that looked so fragile that they might simply blow away at any moment. These contradictions at the very origins of modernism are a powerful counter to a view of architecture as a profoundly positive activity. Furthermore, these ancestors of modernism present a challenge to the narrative of the ruin. Their transience, their fragility and weakness were all qualities that were already present in the buildings from the very beginning; rather than leaving behind a distressed mass of concrete, they have tended to disappear without trace, leaving nothing behind but ephemera. We will see that these buildings were both already ruined, but also never able to become ruins, and we will assess how this self-contradictory condition affects our understanding of architecture as monument and memory. It will be argued that the strange fragility and lack of monumentality of the iron & glass palaces is a quality that contributed to, even encouraged, their failure, and we will examine the implications this realisation might have for architectural culture.

In light of the new lessons learned in our historical study of these architectural failures we will also examine a number of movements supposedly carrying on the technological tradition of modernism, using the new insights to critique supposedly radical streams of contemporary architecture. The analysis of the iron & glass buildings and their failure will show that far from a continuous legacy of radical modernism, the problems of architecture and its relationship to culture and technology that they posed are still unresolved today; in fact, it will be argued that we are as far away from a revolutionary architecture now as we were at the time the iron & glass buildings emerged.

Iron & Glass

The Great Conservatory at Chatsworth House,
Joseph Paxton & Decimus Burton, 1841

Of all cultural forms, architectural modernism was perhaps the modernism most directly influenced by specific technological developments. Unlike literature, whose technologies of creation and dissemination remained more or less same from the 19th to the 20th centuries, or music, whose late 19th century development in recording technology – phonography – would be embraced most quickly in the field of popular music, modernism in architecture can effectively be traced back to two events – the development of mass-produced cast iron & plate glass. And again, unlike in literature and music, whose modernisms worked primarily with form and technique, architectural modernism became an ideology in which the industrial would play a most important role. One way to understand this condition is that it is due to the fact that of all cultural forms, architecture is the one that requires the largest amounts of capital to produce; not only

4

the huge masses of material that must be assembled, but also the huge amounts of labour that go into the erection of buildings. If we (not unproblematically) think of architecture as an art form, then it is the art form that is still most directly tied to its patrons, with all the ideological problems that entails. With this in mind, it is understandable that the effects of 19th century technological advances, the new materials and new methods of fabrication, as well as other factors such as rapid urbanisation, and changing political and economic cultures would be felt more deeply in the discipline of architecture than in any other cultural form; and also why modernism in architecture would have such a close and complex relationship to technological advancement.

Although modernist architecture is generally considered to originate in the early 20th century, histories generally point towards the earliest origins of modernism as being the iron & glass revolution in the 19th century; what would later become modernist shibboleths such as honesty in construction, truth to materials, the stripping back of decoration and a commitment to mass-manufacturing and pre-fabrication were all presaged in the engineering achievements of the 19th century, and the 'engineer-geniuses' of the time, such as Gustave Eiffel and Isambard Kingdom Brunel, are better publicly remembered than any architects of their time. Against the historicism of the bourgeois academy, and in contrast to aestheticians merely horrified by the effects of industrialisation (such as A.N.W. Pugin), some 19th century theorists such as Eugene Violet-le-Duc saw in raw engineering a more honest, more rational expression of the problems of a rapidly changing society. The conventional reading of the iron & glass building phenomenon is that it allowed a new architectural method to develop: while it was ignored by the prevailing 'academic' minds, who thought of the structures as 'mere' engineering, the increasing complexity and demands of building typologies led to iron & glass being the medium in which a new kind of space emerged; thus conceptually suturing the form to notions of progress. This conceptual symbiosis led to the materials and their methods of application becoming symbolic of their age.

Iron & glass buildings first started to be built soon before the start of the 19th century, mostly by gardeners rather than architects or engineers. These mainly consisted of lean-to roofs, functioning as *orangeries* for private residences. Constructed of sash bars and supported against masonry walls, these were simple structures, considered entirely as vignettes within the sequence of rooms and spaces of the houses to which they were attached.[1] Up until the middle of the century ferro-vitreous architectural technology developed with the construction of larger and larger winter gardens and greenhouses, and the working out of problems such as vaulted iron roofs or the construction of bridges. When cast-iron technology first emerged it was trapped in the patterns of stone and wood; the Iron Bridge (1781-) in Shropshire is an almost direct translation of timber construction into the new material.

There are two main families of ferro-vitreous building – those of a 'mixed' construction, in which an iron & glass roof structure was constructed within a standard masonry building, and those which we might call 'pure' construction, where apart from the foundations, the building has no masonry aspect. It should be acknowledged that there were varying degrees between these two positions; structurally there is no such thing as a 'pure' iron & glass building, the distinction is an aesthetic one. 'Pure' construction reveals the iron & glass, 'mixed' construction conceals it from the exterior view. As well as this aesthetic distinction, there are, basically speaking, five different types of ferro-vitreous architecture: railway stations, arcades, department stores, winter gardens, and exhibition palaces. All of these are typologies whose construction only became possible with the introduction of iron & glass; they all represent genuinely *new* forms of space, forms that are all linked by their *transience*.[2]

The grand *railway stations* were mostly built during the craze of speculative railway building that occurred in the latter half of the 19th century, and are perhaps the most commonly surviving of all the ferro-vitreous buildings. The railway boom is perhaps the technological advance that most changed the way 19th century space was experienced; it brought to the world unprecedented velocity, distance and size. The extruded railway sheds were among the most impressive examples of engineering of their time, but were without exception hidden behind a building constructed in an acceptable architectural mode. They represented solutions to new problems that could not be solved within the constraints of an academic architectural style, but it was considered inappropriate for them to exist on their own, especially within an urban context. Those contemporary critics not immediately repulsed by industrial architecture spoke of the success with which the 'Architecture' of the building expressed or resolved the 'Engineering' part, regarding the tension between the quantifiable and the ineffable.[3] But these were not equally weighted terms; by separating the two registers of meaning in the building, efforts were made to protect the *knowledge* of the architect – as the engineer had nothing to do but solve the problem as it was presented to them, their 'solution' could never be Architecture, which had the more difficult task of *expressing* what it did; of communicating its purpose by making a statement within an already established language, to which access was restricted. This insoluble tension between the ideal polarities of function and communication, and the way in which professional anxieties are drawn within it is something we shall return to again in this study.

Arcades were even more concealed than the railway stations. Basic roofs covering small shopping streets, these were amongst the earliest ferro-vitreous structures built, and were common in the cities of Old-Europe. At first spaces inhabited by the early bourgeoisie, they would often later become the haunts of prostitutes and vagabonds. Although in many cities they are entirely lost, there are still places in which the more salubrious of the arcades have survived; usually when they were of larger or grander scale, for example the Galleria Vittorio Emanuele II (1867-) in Milan or the arcades of Leeds. In Walter Benjamin's work *The Arcades Project*, the arcades are lenses through which the birth of modern capitalist culture is examined. Arcades were the perfect haunts of the *flâneur*, that transient wanderer of the city whose disinterested gaze foresaw the passive modern consumer. For Benjamin, the arcades are manifestations of the *phantasmagorias* of modernity, neither interior nor exterior spaces. The arcades may have been the original spaces in which the exchange value of the commodity came to prominence, but for Benjamin they also are the locus of fragments of latent potential; a utopian spark which he often identifies as residing in the germinal iron construction of their roofs.[4] Benjamin was writing in the context of the disappearance of most of the Paris arcades; he was making the case for a radical reappraisal of what even in the 1930s was a lost culture; indeed, those arcades that still exist are imbued with a sense of being adrift out of time, dwarfed by the spaces and cultures that they inaugurated.

The *department stores* were the grand offspring of the arcades; products of a blossoming bourgeoisie and the culture of conspicuous consumption that they cultivated, this peculiar typology resulted in buildings of effectively open-plan 'free' space filled with independent commercial units, held behind massive facades that gave off an impression of an often-gaudy grandeur. The contradiction between the aspirations of consumption and the methods by which it could be achieved resulted in buildings such as *le Bon Marché* in Paris (1867-), often acknowledged as the first of the type. This particular architectural technique would later develop into the office building with a cast-iron frame, which further tended towards the proto-skyscrapers of Louis Sullivan and others in the US. In many ways arcades and department stores continue to be built; of all the iron & glass buildings their influence is most easily discerned in the axial arrangements and roof-lit avenues of the ubiquitous shopping malls; a steroidal typology, prone to gigantism. Although much maligned by lovers of the small shop and also those who find consumerist homogeneity depressing, it has to be admitted that they are also extremely popular spaces, as long as we understand popular to mean frequently constructed and often visited.

Winter gardens were massive greenhouses, built at first in the grounds of country estates, but later constructed in parks as public works. These were the first examples of a ferro-vitreous architecture that was not reliant on substantial masonry structures or conventional architecture as support or mask; this nakedness was 'permissible' partly because architects were rarely involved in their design, but also because the structures were constructed out of the way from other buildings; in a large garden setting there was no real architectural ensemble to be a part of, in fact, the dominant ensemble was the 'nature' within and the 'nature' without. The winter gardens were museums of nature; within their glass walls the arboreal products of the world were arranged, catalogued and preserved – plants were collected from around the world in much the same way as cultural artefacts.[5] A great number of these structures were built in the second half of the 19th century, and a number of outstanding examples survive, such as at Kew, Vienna, or Brussels. Although these spaces are among the only ways one can now truly appreciate the fantastic qualities of iron & glass architecture, the vast majority of winter gardens of the 19th century are long gone, victims of neglect and short-sighted demolition:

> Whereas stylistic architecture recapitulated history, the builders of the glasshouses had to conceive designs for

contents that were ephemeral – plants or exhibitions. The trend toward the temporary was inherent in the plant houses and the exhibition buildings, and it expressed itself in the construction. Not suitable for industry and serving only for exhibitions or recreation, many of the glasshouses were left to decay, unappreciated, in less than a decade.[6]

But by far the most bizarre and fantastic of the ferro-vitreous proto-modernist structures have to be the *Exhibition Palaces*. Beginning with the virtually unprecedented Crystal Palace (1851), designed by Joseph Paxton for the Great Exhibition in London, a strange, ambitious, deliriously optimistic and naively short-sighted typology was born. Over the next fifty years these would create some of the most incredible moments in architectural history, yet almost all now exist only as archive material. The Great Exhibition itself is thought of as the event that marked the birth of modern consumer-capitalist culture, with its effect of 'putting the world on display'; and it sparked a copycat series of exhibitions around the world, such as the 1889 Paris Exhibition or the 1893 Columbian Exhibition in Chicago, to name but two.

Why have they disappeared? Of all the buildings built for the 19th century world's fairs, only the Eiffel Tower (1889-) is significantly standing. Almost all of the exhibition buildings themselves are gone, leaving nothing but ephemera, photographs and place names. Admittedly, they were often designed as temporary structures, but in a large number of cases after the exhibitions had run there were vigorous attempts made to make the buildings permanent, often in the guise of 'Palaces for the People'. In these cases, it was mostly fire or financial ruin that eventually claimed them.

In the following sections I will discuss three examples of the ferro-vitreous glass palaces. Firstly the original Crystal Palace at Hyde Park (1851), will be discussed both in terms of its conventional architectural significance and its related but generally scholarly distinct cultural significance. The rebuilt Crystal Palace at Sydenham (1854-1936), which is rarely properly separated out historically from the Hyde Park building, will be discussed in terms of its fantastic architecture and its overall failure, while the almost completely unremembered Albert Palace (1885-92) will be discussed with regard to its melancholic life and death and its relationship to architectural memory.

The Crystal Palace at Hyde Park

Joseph Paxton's ferro-vitreous edifice for the *Great Exhibition of the Works of Industry of all Nations* is undoubtedly the most famous of all of the 19th century exhibition palaces. Pejoratively nicknamed the 'Crystal Palace' before it was even built, it swiftly became the subject of great affection and adulation, and is now widely regarded as a masterpiece of architectural design.[7] Unlike some other events featured in this book, the Great Exhibition generated a vast body of written and graphic material, a very large amount of which still exists. In recent years it has generated much discussion as well, a great many articles and books being published on it. This production has peaked at anniversaries, especially those at which exhibitions paying explicit homage were held (1951, 2000). Despite this wealth of material, the memory of the Crystal Palace is somewhat diffuse, scattered into myriad different narratives and positions, which broadly speaking we can describe as falling within the space between three extreme positions.

The first of these is the popular/populist view, which sees the Great Exhibition as the source of great pride, a flourishing of Victorian genius and technological prowess, the birth of liberal modernity. This view is of course most commonly held in the UK itself, where there is still great popular nostalgia for the period when Britain was a world power, and when it led the world in technological development and the liberality of its capitalist culture. Needless to say, this attitude to the exhibition is most often held by conservatives who do not blanche at making appeals to the greatness of empires and all that went with them. This view is a naïve one; it takes the pronouncements of those involved in the creation of the exhibition, such as Prince Albert, at face value, without delving any further.

The second attitude is the scholarly view: the last twenty years have seen the emergence of a revisionist narrative of the history of the Great Exhibition which has drawn out and focused upon various other narratives to the official, laudatory one, most obviously the stories and responses of those foreigners, women and workers who attended, but also drawing out the multifarious attitudes towards the exhibition from within the upper classes at whom its rhetoric was mostly aimed. This scholarly attitude stresses the heterogeneity of cultural meanings that the exhibition generated, emphasizing its conflicting and contradictory nature, breaking up, at least at the academic level, the dominant narrative that existed previously.

The third attitude can be described as the technological, or architectural attitude, which sees the Crystal Palace from a distance, viewed through the lens of later developments in the culture of architecture and building. Generally lacking anything more than cursory cultural observations, the technological view of the Crystal Palace is as a masterful solution; the first building to truly make genuine use of the mass-production technologies newly available at the time, a presaging of future methods of spatial production and a testament to the mindset of the problem-solving designer.

It would be impossible here to offer up a comprehensive new mix of these ways of looking at the Great Exhibition, which would be a far larger project than the one undertaken here, but at the same time with regard to what follows I cannot proceed without at least providing some brief analysis of the event. In that case the following will attempt to contrast the scholarly and architectural approaches, which often have existed in almost complete isolation from each other.

Industrial exhibitions of one kind or another had been held for at least half a century before 1851.[8] However, as the Great Exhibition would be the first that was international in any sense, and as it would also be an event on a scale that dwarfed any previous exhibition, then it is not unreasonable to think of it in terms of a 'first of its kind'. Moreover, it set in motion a massive cultural movement; the Great Exhibition is often said to be the birth of modern capitalist culture, both in terms of the promotion of ideologies of free trade and competitive display but also in the new ways in which objects were consumed, and how they were seen. Benjamin refers to how the exhibitions were 'training schools in which the masses, barred from consuming, learned empathy with exchange value',[9] while more recently Peter Sloterdijk would write that with the Great Exhibition, 'a new aesthetic of immersion began its triumphal procession through modernity'.[10] The financial success of the Great Exhibition was swiftly emulated: both New York and Paris would hold their own exhibitions within the next five years, and there would be a great many others held throughout the century all over the world. As time went on, the event would slowly metamorphose into what is now known as the 'Expo', a strange shadow counterpart to the events of so long ago, but one that still occurs, albeit fitfully, and with a strange, undead quality to it. By the time the first half-century of exhibitions was over the crystalline behemoths of the early exhibitions had been replaced by the 'pavilion' format, whereby countries, firms and even movements would construct miniature ideological edifices to their own projected self identities. The 1900 Paris exhibition was the first to truly embrace this format, and in future years one could encounter such seminal works of architecture such as Melnikov's Soviet Pavilion and Le Corbusier's Pavilion Esprit Nouveau (Paris 1925), Mies van der Rohe's Barcelona Pavilion (Barcelona 1929), Le Corbusier & Iannis Xenakis' Phillips Pavilion (Brussels 1958), or witness the desperately tragic face-off between Albert Speer and Boris Iofan (Paris 1937). Much later, important buildings by Buckminster Fuller and Moshe Safdie (Montreal 1967) would occasionally be created, but generally the trend has been for the Expo to decline in significance as both a trade fair and ideological display as the years have progressed. However, 2010 saw an Expo held in

Shanghai, China. This was technically the largest ever, presumably as governments are looking to stimulate trade relationships with newly-powerful China, but overall it wasa rather confused expression of the eclecticism of contemporary architecture.

The Crystal Palace was commissioned in 1849 as part of the plans for an international exhibition of arts and manufactures dreamt up by Albert, the Prince Consort, and Henry Cole, the head of the Royal Society for the Encouragement of Arts, Manufactures and Commerce. In the words of Prince Albert:

> The Exhibition of 1851 is to give us a true test and a living picture of the point of development at which the whole of mankind has arrived [...] and a new starting point from which all nations will be able to direct their future exertions.[11]

In the exhibition was to be the largest collection of objects yet assembled; from the largest to the smallest, from raw materials to traditional crafts, to industrial machinery and sculpture. It was to be a gigantic display cabinet in which the world would examine itself in the spirit of mutual development and brotherly competition, but it was also to be a gloating display of the leading position that the UK had attained in terms of industrial development.

The story of how the building came about is almost legendary; a competition was held to which there were almost 250 entries, none of which could fulfil the needs of the Exhibition Committee who required a building of vast scale which was also cheap, temporary, and light on the ground. The committee themselves (including I.K. Brunel) then drew up a rather hapless design of masonry, iron & glass, which was essentially no better. Enter Joseph Paxton, who as head gardener at the stately home Chatsworth House had already created one of the largest ferro-vitreous structures yet built. He prepared his own concept for the building on a single piece of blotting paper, which he showed to the committee to little effect: they were reportedly somewhat unconvinced by his proposal, or at least unconvinced in his ability to achieve it. After this setback he made the very astute political move of publishing his own proposal in a press already ill-disposed to the design of the committee (due to its apparent permanence in the context of much loved Hyde Park). By aligning himself with popular opinion (and also by offering the only proposal that came within the budget), he secured the commission, and was involved with the project all the way through from the beginning to the final stages.

The Crystal Palace in Hyde Park, Joseph Paxton,1851

The rest is of the story is well documented. The Crystal Palace was erected in a matter of four months, stood proudly for six months, during which time over six million people passed through its doors to look at more than one-hundred-thousand exhibits from almost fifteen-thousand separate exhibitors, ranging from fully functioning industrial machinery to raw materials, from a knife with over one hundred blades to the Koh-I-Noor diamond itself, and including a seemingly limitless amount of furniture, products and objects. The experience was overwhelming: 'It was like – like nothing but itself, unsur-passable, indescribable, unique, amazing, real!' (*Tallis' History and Description of the Crystal Palace*). It would seem to be difficult to overestimate its significance; a famous illustration by George Cruikshank shows *All the World Going to the Great Exhibition*, the planet covered in people swarming towards the Crystal Palace, which sits upon the globe like a crown – in many ways the Great Exhibition was the first time that a single event had conceptually incorporated the *entire world*.

The form that most dominated the Crystal Palace as an archi-tectural composition was the vaulted transept at the centre, which is now the most iconically reproduced image of the palace. This vault, with its delicate fan details has become the general signifier of 'Crystal Palace'-ness, the logo of the building, if you will. The form of Paxton's design was not, as might be assumed, originally based upon his famous Great Conservatory at Chatsworth (1836-1920), with its double sprung roof and vaulted arrangement. He had also designed a 'roof and furrow' system for a greenhouse built to hold a *Victoria Regia* lily, from the ribbed leaves of which he (in an oft-repeated anecdote) apparently drew structural inspiration. This greenhouse was relatively small, box-like and supported on columns; Paxton's original design for the Crystal Palace was born of a module he devised from this previous structure, constrained to the largest panes of glass that could be built at that time. Out of this module he devised a structural grid of cast iron columns 24ft apart that was repeated in three dimensions (the columns were also 24ft high). He then extruded the grid out to a size that would accom-modate all of the required space, while also having it as close to the symbolic length of 1851ft as possible. And that was that.

The simplicity of the design is of course remarkable, the product of the most unpretentious thinking, focused upon a single task at hand. There was a problem; nobody had yet managed to solve it, and Paxton stepped in as the only man who could do the job. It's doubtful that anybody has solved a brief that heroically since, and in many ways his story is paradigmatic of the no-nonsense Victorian self-made genius, a character that is as popular now as it ever has been. What he created, perhaps due to his 'outsider' status as neither an architect nor an engineer, was a design that at the time would not have been recognised as architectural at all; as previously mentioned, the architectural 'academy' made a strong and somewhat aggressive distinction between architecture and engineering. Although it's true that the theoretical systems of architecture at the time were unable to accommodate such unprecedented design, it's difficult not to see this distinction as a desperate one, born of the realisation that industrialisation had arrived, and not only was not going away but was actually accelerating. The resulting protectionism of knowledge, exemplified by the denigration of design that proceeded without initiation into the 'styles' is one born of fear; a patently absurd barrier, leading to logical contortions whereby the most efficiently engineered shed expresses its 'shed-ness' less well than an architect's ornamented, aestheticised offering, which is capable of a deeper, more meaningful portrayal of an ideal of 'efficiency'. Put simply – when threatened, it is more important to signify than to be.

The Crystal Palace building itself became deeply iconic, which is strange considering that the design was so minimal, being almost nothing more than a large glass cabinet in which the objects and people inside were displayed. People had never experienced a building of such transparency and immateriality before, indeed, this transparency was frequently overwhelming. One might perhaps expect that it would be difficult for something famous for its very lack of visual presence to become a visual icon, but there is perhaps a reason for this. Part of the public opposition to the competition designs was based on the location of the building in Hyde Park; many were aghast at the idea of a heavy structure on the land at all, and in this way

Paxton's light and obviously temporary design pleased them. But their opposition went further – there were a number of mature elm trees on the site, and public pressure forced the committee to demand of Paxton changes to the design that would allow the trees to be retained. It was at this point that the famous transept was added to the design, thus giving the building not only an iconic exterior form that would be memorable long after its physical absence, but also the picturesque image of majestic trees contained within a vault – an architectural form with explicit historical resonances. Here a speculation is appropriate: to what extent does the memory of the Crystal Palace rely upon it having such a 'composition'? Kenneth Frampton outlines the memory of the Crystal Palace from the technological perspective when he writes that 'The Crystal Palace was not so much a particular form as it was a building process made manifest as a total system, from its initial conception, fabrication and trans-shipment, to its final erection and dismantling'.[12] But it was also the particular form of the transept roof, as documented in postcards, drawings and photographs that made the palace memorable at all – contemporary commentators noted that the transept did much to bring the palace to the level of 'Architecture' – compare Frampton's reading to the more contemporary view of Fergusson:

As first proposed, the Hyde Park Crystal Palace, though an admirable piece of Civil Engineering, had no claim to be considered as an architectural design. Use, and use only, pervaded every arrangement, and it was not ornamented to such an extent as to elevate it into the class of Fine Arts. The subsequent introduction of the arched transept with the consequent arrangements at each end and on each side, did much to bring it within that category.[13]

If the palace had actually been as featureless as the original design suggested, if it was as obviously and simply nothing more than a 'system', as the original drawings showed, as the later Glass Palace at Munich (1853-1931) would tend towards, then what effect would it have had? It's impossible to say, although perhaps it would have been a less memorable icon, and a more 'truthful' influence on rationalist architecture in years to come. What is definitely clear however is that even at this early stage of proto-functionalism, there are always questions of the aesthetic, the memorable or the communicative at work. In much the same way that academic architects were dealing in ideals of architectural meaning, the technological reading of the Crystal Palace is also positing an ideal picture of totally non-aesthetic functioning. Architecture cannot help but be significant.

In this study we will be often focusing on the relationship of the architecture discussed to its mediation; architecture's complex conceptual ties to memory will be seen to be problematic when conditions of ephemerality are involved. If I may be permitted to introduce theoretical terminology, I will use the word 'spectrality'[14] to describe the inconsistent presence of objects and their mediated being. Jacques Derrida once argued that "the structure of the archive is spectral", meaning that the marks we make are inextricably bound up with a logic of ghosts, that representation is in itself haunted, as in the ghostly trace of human presence, but also that our own haunted finitude is made clear in the making of the mark. In short, our history is the history of our own haunting. Derrida - as a thinker of the archive or of the 'body of knowledge' - argued that the ghost was a more appropriate figure for our being than any fully present human subject: instead of ontology, he proposed a *hauntology*. But this was not an entirely abstract or poetic observation; it describes a concrete condition. We can expand upon Derrida's statement thus: all media, in some way, are spectral. All marks made create a fragmented image of the human who inscribes them. Almost every medium of communication or transmission – from writing to telephony to television and beyond – proliferates spectral images that create fragments out of single identities. Although architecture is usually seen as the epitome of solidity, and indeed draws much of its power from its potential to long outlast its builders, we will return time and again to ways in which architecture itself is spectral. In the case of the Crystal Palace, this spectrality was partly manifested by the fact that it was constructed almost entirely from glass, a material not only transparent, but one that multiplies and fragments images. Contemporary accounts focused on the strange and unsettling experience of being within such an immaterial space: 'Glass could stand in for the invisible nature of mediation in complex, "modern," nineteenth-century experience: [...] Glass's unreadability, insistently spectral, insistently material, pressed upon the cultural imaginary'.[15]

Beyond this there is another level of spectrality; the fact that the Crystal Palace was quickly and cleanly removed from its site leaving nothing but its buried foundations means that we only experience the building in its mediated form; it is preserved but at a distance, as fragments. It actually plays a significant historical role in this regard; inside the Great Exhibition was one of the very first exhibitions of photography, and the Crystal Palace itself was photographed extensively in a way that was unprecedented; architectural photography effectively begins here. The rapid disappearance of the Crystal Palace emphasized its success; it existed only in its glorious prime; something that cannot be said for its later incarnation. As an ephemeral object (albeit on a massive scale), it was saved the ignominy of struggling to be a success for more than a few months.

The Crystal Palace was the first (and one of the only) financial successes of the world exhibitions. At first they were run as genuinely commercial concerns, but by the beginning of the 20th century their trade and propaganda value began to be its own reward, with the hosts and participants all taking part for a loss.

The Great Exhibition in the Crystal Palace

The Great Exhibition specifically, and the world exhibitions in general were rhetorically structured around themes of brotherhood and progress. Brotherhood, as all the peoples of the world would supposedly be drawn closer by the spirit of collaboration, display and free trade that was embodied by exhibitions, and progress, as the plenitude of comparative displays were supposed to testify to the bright future that the onward march of technology was bringing forth. Prince Albert spoke of '...a period of most wonderful transition, which tends rapidly to accomplish that great end, to which, indeed, all history points – the realization of the unity of mankind'.[16] Although in the case of the Great Exhibition, the fact that Great Britain occupied by far the largest space was intended to stress that said brotherhood did not necessarily mean equality. In fact, the Great Exhibition was a massive and somewhat histrionic display of Britain's 'greatness'; it was 'the self-authored portrait of a self-universalizing people'.[17] with professions of peace juxtaposed with displays of weaponry; talk of brotherhood alongside celebrations of imperial exploitation.

But at the same time, where there is self-aggrandisement, fear and doubt is never far away – the Great Exhibition being held in 1851 cannot help but bring forth images of revolutions and insurgency. The Great Exhibition was being organized and formulated in the wake of the failed European revolutions of 1848, and in the UK, the Chartists and the Anti-Corn Law movement threatened to unleash the same turmoil on British soil. In this context the Great Exhibition has been understood as a 'counter-revolutionary measure',[18] as a symbolic plaster over open social wounds, but it was also moving in the direction of economic and political liberalization; 'it offered the tantalizing prospect of implicitly supporting free trade but distracting the public from revolution'.[19] It was a path between a volatile working class and a protectionist aristocracy. It is well documented that before the exhibition there were all kinds of worries – of assassinations, of terrorism, of petty violence, of disease, of infrastructural collapse, but it is equally well documented that the exhibition passed without any violence or even significant disruption; the hordes of anarchists failed to materialize.

Overall, the Crystal Palace was certainly one of the most significant early moments of modern capitalism – indeed, it is widely described as *the* moment in which modern (or even *postmodern)* capitalist culture was born, the point at which the gaze of capitalism first turned back upon itself and the symbolic value of the products that it was consuming; the very beginnings of 'the spectacle'. It is naïve for the Crystal Palace to be understood merely as the first example of the deployment of large-scale prefabrication in architecture: it is important that all of the contradictory issues that relate to it are understood to be as much *architectural* issues as any other kind.

The Crystal Palace at Sydenham

One of the things most often misunderstood about the Crystal Palace is that there were two different incarnations of the building, and that the two buildings were very different in terms of form, setting, purpose, reception and achievement. The two palaces are often conflated as one single cultural event, and yet their residues of meaning are incredibly different. In the following section I intend to properly introduce the Sydenham Crystal Palace, and describe some of the strange architectural and cultural effects of the ill-fated ferro-vitreous edifice. We have already seen that despite the incredible successes of the Great Exhibition it was the scene of much doubt, but in the Sydenham Palace we will see a fantasy architecture, significantly removed from the proto-functionalism of its predecessor, and a number of fragments of a modern architectural melancholy.

Before the Great Exhibition had even shut its gates there were public discussions ongoing about what fate would befall the building. There was absolutely no question of the building being retained upon the land on which it stood, but opinion was split as to what its fate should be. There were those who felt that as the Exhibition had been such a resounding success, it would be a terrible shame not to retain the building and have some permanent reminder of the wonders of the exhibition, as well as a permanent facility for the health and edification of the public. On the other hand, in a view reminiscent of the attitudes of later radicals like Cedric Price, it was argued that as the palace had been a mere functional artefact, a massive display cabinet, there would be no point keeping it once its purpose was served.[20] A number of strange proposals were made, displayed and discussed through the popular and the architectural press. These included the preposterous notion of stacking up the cubic iron modules to create a 'Crystal Tower' 1000ft high,[21] or rather

24

audacious proposals to massively extend the palace right where it stood in Hyde Park. Owen Jones proposed the re-use of the material from the palace to create a 'Palace of the People' on Muswell Hill in North London (later the home of the Alexandra Palace, which was actually built with the remains of the much ignored 1862 International Exhibition).[22] This would have been built atop a new railway station, and would have been heavily oriented towards commerce – a transit hub/shopping centre configuration that would have effectively been the paradigm for many an inner-city development in future. Prince Albert himself suggested that the Crystal Palace be rebuilt on the recently laid-out Battersea Park to be used as a winter garden, an idea to which we shall return.[23]

In the end, however, it was Joseph Paxton who again managed to set the future of the palace. Towards the end of the exhibition he became a director of the Crystal Palace Company which had been formed with the sole purpose of re-building the Crystal Palace as the centrepiece of a large formal garden on Sydenham Hill to the south of London. Through the sale of shares they swiftly managed to raise the £500,000 required, and

The Crystal Palace at Sydenham, Joseph Paxton,1854

so the palace was Paxton's again, being taken down, transported, re-erected and open to the public again by 1854.

At this point it is worth analysing the physical differences between the two palaces. As we have seen, the Hyde Park Palace was a remarkably clear solution to a problem that was mostly defined by cost and time – the budget was low, the schedule tight, and none of the other designs were plausible in the context. But that is not to say that its brilliant simplicity was even something that Paxton was particularly proud of – while making the case for his Sydenham proposal, he denigrated the original Exhibition building as 'the simplest, the merest mechanical building that could be made'.[24] This lack of confidence in what would later be thought of as the building's purity was more than made evident by the building that was eventually designed. Where the Hyde Park Palace was mostly a shed, enlivened by a single large transept, the new palace at Sydenham had vaults that ran the entire length of the nave, with a transept of equal height at each end of the building, and a new, extra large transept in the middle. The new building was, contrary to popular misconception, both shorter (1848/1608 ft.) and slimmer (408/312 ft.) than the Great Exhibition building, but it was substantially loftier (up to six storeys compared to two for the Hyde Park Palace);[25] thus appearing much larger, and its arrangement was far more 'composed', far more 'architectural'. At the time this was considered a great improvement, as described by Fergusson:

> As re-erected at Sydenham, the building has far greater claims to rank among the important architectural objects of the world. [...] Nothing can well be better, or better subordinated, than the great and two minor transepts joined together by the circular roofs of the naves, and the whole arrangement is such as to produce the most pleasing effects both internally and externally.[26]

However, to contemporary eyes it tends to look like somewhat of a retreat, a shrinking back from a premonition of systems to come. The introduction of 'proper' architectural proportions to the building, as well as a hierarchy of differing vaults looks like a rejection of the simplicity of the original, especially when set out in its grandiose gardens. There was more to this redesign than simply adding in as much extra 'Architecture' as the budget would allow, however – the conception of what the palace was to be used for was completely different:

> In taking the structure of the Exhibition of 1851 – that type of a class of architecture which may fairly be called "Modern English" – as the model for the building at Sydenham, the projectors found it necessary to make such modifications and improvements as were suggested by the difference between a temporary receiving house for the world's industrial wealth, and a permanent Palace of Art and Education.[27]

As opposed to being a temporary spectacle of the consumption of images of production, the relocated Crystal Palace was to fit into the category of buildings for the edification and uplift of the people. Much like the museums of 'Albertopolis' (an area of Kensington to the south of Hyde Park which was purchased with the proceeds of the Great Exhibition, and upon which a number of large museums and public facilities would be built), the Sydenham Palace was to be a true 'Palace for the People' where all social classes could relax in an environment of education and culture. This has much in common with then-contemporary rational recreation movements, whereby 'the masses' were to be 'improved' by being drawn away from their own disgusting situation and given the chance to become better people. This was to be achieved partially through exposure to culture and educational pursuits, partially through being placed in situations where inequity was unavailable to them, and partially through exposure to the 'better classes'. Of course this 'improvement' was also intended to neutralise the threat that an organised working class could pose to the establishment, so although the palace was supposedly of genuine benefit to the working classes, they were still subject to the patronising and condescending attitudes of the middle and upper classes.

The charter of the Crystal Palace Company enshrined the notion that it was a building for the use of the 'common' people, and that it was to be educational on a number of levels.[28] At the very far northern end of the building were a number of rooms set aside for not just rational recreation but for genuine higher education, albeit of a segregated kind: this was the Crystal Palace School of Art, Science and Literature.[29] Within this small institution there was a library, a lecture theatre, and classrooms for female students of fine arts, music and literature, and male students of engineering. Bearing in mind that at around the same time a design school was founded in the Victoria & Albert museum that would eventually become the Royal College of Art, another direct offshoot of the Great Exhibition, then it is tantalising to consider the educational atmosphere of attending art school in this ferro-vitreous palace; certainly, it was seen as a huge benefit to have access to the collections of sculpture and art for studying. The school would in fact still be functioning beyond the end of the Sydenham Palace's life, with studios in one of the large water towers that flanked the building and powered its fountains.

If the Hyde Park Palace can be seen as a gigantic display case, setting the paradigm for all manner of spatial cultures to come, then the Sydenham Palace was a structure with a much more strange and surreal set of spaces, which bear further description. As opposed to the notion that the Sydenham Palace was an inferior architectural statement, I suggest that the spatial and cultural effects of the rebuilt palace were even stranger than the original, creating a strange hybrid that was as connected to

The Crystal Palace interior, c.1860

romanticism as modernism; suggesting a dreamy synthesis of the two. The whole edifice was laid out with fountains and plants, with trees and a proliferation of climbing plants such as ivy wrapping their way up towards the roof. Although it was filled with flora, this was not to the extent to which it could be honestly classed a winter garden – there were far too many other functions occurring in the palace, too much other programme for it to be a building *about* foliage. The spatial quality of a winter garden usually involves the recession of the building to create a pseudo-natural environment, with a series of paths in amongst a planted space. In the case of the Sydenham Palace, the area dedicated to plants was comparatively small, and thus the foliage could not dominate the building, it grew around it and up it, without ever overwhelming it.

Rather than a pure exhibition palace or winter garden, or even a simple hybrid of the two, the primary spatial experience of the Sydenham Palace was rather more that of a strange proto-virtual reality, primarily due to the system of courts. It cannot be stressed just how strange this collection of spaces actually was, a complex mixture of what Venturi & Scott Brown would later describe as the 'duck' and 'decorated shed'; neither truthful nor entirely false, an eerie collage of strange spatial juxtapositions.[30] The court system was an attempt to create within the palace an immersive educational environment by constructing actual-size replicas of various historical architectural styles throughout the building. There were over twenty-five individual courts originally constructed in the palace, each representing a specific architectural style ranging from antiquity to recent times.[31] One could visit the Egyptian, Alhambra or Greek courts, or three varieties of medieval court – French, English and German. One could enter a replica of a Roman villa from Pompeii, or stand before a wooden screen depicting all of the Kings and Queens of England. In some ways the method of curation is familiar from many a 19th century museum, but the way in which the viewer, rather than engaging with an object across a display, entered fully into the exhibit is surely unique.[32] But this immersion was never total – some of the courts were fully closed, with a ceiling and floor in keeping with their theme, but the girders of the palace would come slicing through the walls, entering and exiting the space to either side as part of an over-arching grid. In other spaces this effect would be even more prominent, as the quasi-masonry walls of the court would simply end at the cornice, revealing the structure above and all around, as if the roof had been lifted right off. Standing in a room of modest proportions, the visitor would have a clear space of many metres above them, the light and sounds of the entire palace reverberating around. Entire courts would be covered in ivy, the circulation routes would pass under the crossed tie-beams that tensioned the structure, which themselves would be overgrown with ivy. Overall, the effect would have been that of a number of distinct spatial logics all competing, in some cases disjunctively co-existing with each other in the same space; an iron girder clashing with an Egyptian column; the seeming solidity of the walls compared with the timber floor creaking three stories up in the air. Even though there are a great many examples of 'dishonest' architecture in this fashion, for example; the Columbian Exhibition in 1893 was notable for the mock-massive structures draped over the iron inside, what is notable here is the fact that there was no attempt being made to create a seamless environment. The Sydenham Palace's fragmentary displays of historical form mimicked in their arrangement the incompleteness of memory, in such a way that the structural grid can be seen as a metaphor for the substratum of memory itself, a 'mystic writing pad';[33] an almost non-existent memory layer that becomes gradually filled with the impressions of objects and recollection. As one commentator described the experience of visiting the palace:

> We are wafted into a region still more dreamlike than anything which even fond memory had retained of the past [...] Hour after hour finds us in wandering mazes lost – the sport of impressions gone as soon as formed, all rapid, vivid, but fleeting.[34]

The courts are in an indeterminate condition between being spaces and objects within space; this overlapping complexity of spatial register was almost unknown again until it reappeared in different guises in both the indeterminate 'plug-in' architecture and the experiments of deconstructivism in the 1970s, both of which we will consider later. Yet here it was occurring in the 1850s; all the hallmarks are there; different registers of structure set against each other, a logic of incompleteness, where no spatial system manages to 'seal' itself off, and, here one can only surmise, an uncanny sense of space. Unlike the Great Exhibition, with its regime of the gaze massively multiplied in the display case of the building itself, the Sydenham Palace is even more fragmentary; displayed objects, micro-spaces and the meta-structure of the palace itself all created a cacophony of objects and spaces, irreducibly complex.

The Sheffield Court at the Crystal Palace, c.1860

Both of the two incarnations of the Crystal Palace were home to great amounts of sculpture. In the case of the Great Exhibition this had been due to a decision not to include fine arts as a category, the preference being instead to focus upon industry and applied arts. Sculpture made it into the exhibition as a result, and some of the most significant displays were sculptures, such as the American Hyram Powers' *The Greek Slave*, which, in what might seem an unbearably kitsch touch, was displayed on a rotating pedestal.[35] The Sydenham Palace had a great amount of sculpture displayed inside, ranging from the massive Egyptian figures at one end of the building to the many classical objects on show. Many, like *The Greek Slave*, with its subject matter of a nude chained to a post who is at once both chaste and lascivious, achieved that very Victorian mixture of the naïvely moral and the unseemly.[36] Indeed, the opening of the Sydenham Palace was delayed under puritanical pressure to add plaster fig-leaves to the genitalia of the (specifically male) statuary.[37] Scenes of a very peculiar quality abounded in the Sydenham Palace: extant photographs show images of marble nudes, surrounded by ivy and other unruly plants, with to one side a gothic screen and then in all other directions taut wires and firm columns stretching off into the distance. In this dream-like environment it is easy to imagine an accompanying sense of poetic melancholy, expanding upon this condition of 'technological romanticism': the fragmentary complexity of the immediate, futuristic spatial environment set against the historical scenes, covered in the 'enhanced nature' of the winter garden and the charged eroticism of the art, create a scene that combines recognisable aspects of romantic aesthetics with functionalist and modernist signifiers.

In the journey between Hyde Park and Sydenham, in the move towards semi-permanence, so much of the palace became given over to practices of documentation and archive. Instead of the Great Exhibition's snapshot of the current moment of industrial and capitalist development, the majority of activities originally on offer in the Sydenham Palace involved the immersion of the visitor in displays, in objects of history and of memory. The whole building, in a sense, was a gigantic memory palace, a journey of objects and scenes from various times embedded within this vessel with its spindle-like frame, the outside world blurred away by the dust on the glass (obvious from photographs taken even very early in its life, and worsened later with the introduction of a motor-racing circuit to the park which was surfaced with a layer of ash), the viewer drifting from fragmentary space to fragmentary space. We can understand the stated desire of 'improvement', of education as a way of reducing the threat of common people, but at the same time the building represents a remarkable thrust both towards and away from the idea of permanence. More than any museum, this collage of incomplete spaces from different times, all tied into a space whose character was most ephemeral: surely this is a most appropriate evocation of spatial memory? Riven between two simultaneous yet opposing logics, that of permanence and that of transience, the Sydenham Palace can genuinely be described as *dialectical*; it was fragmented in the manner of what Walter Benjamin calls 'the Ruin': 'Allegories are, in the realm of thoughts, what ruins are in the realm of things'.[38]

To briefly explain; Benjamin identifies allegory as a quality opposed to symbol. In allegory, meaning is fragmented, and through allegory history and its ruptures can be grasped in objects that are apparently simple in their presence. Although Benjamin originally analyses allegory through the figure of the German tragic drama, or *Trauerspiel*, it is for him also a modern phenomenon, particular to the rise of bourgeois capitalist culture in the late 19th century.[39] We can understand it best in this context as the expression of a fragmented, dialectical meaning; as opposed to a totality of symbols, or a complete history, the allegory is destructive; it is tied to melancholy, but also progress:

Allegory has to do, precisely in its destructive furor, with dispelling the illusion that proceeds from all "given order," whether of art or of life: the illusion of totality or of organic wholeness which transfigures that order and makes it seem endurable.[40]

This fragmented notion of meaning and history is inextricably tied to a commitment to radical change; to Benjamin, history is a shifting concatenation of fragments which carry residual latent moments of radical utopian potential. Benjamin identifies the melancholic allegorical sense of history and meaning with the spatial qualities of the fragmented ruin: 'the allegorical physiognomy of the nature-history, which is put on stage in the Trauerspiel, is present in reality in the form of the ruin. In the ruin history has physically merged into the setting'.[41]

I suggest that opposed to the academic architecture of its time, which we might think of as symbolic, the Sydenham Palace can be described as 'allegorical'. The palace was obviously not a ruin in the normal sense of the word; but in its contradictory existence it embodied certain aspects of the condition; the ruin is both a symbol of monumentality in its massive remnants, but it is also a symbol of the inevitable transience of things. At one level of abstraction, the Sydenham Palace's display of objects and the museum-like qualities of its educational displays are tendencies towards memory and archive. On the other hand the fragile weightlessness of its architecture and its incomplete spatial relationships are qualities of disappearance. In this sense the Sydenham Palace, even before its decline, represents an example of what we might call the 'abstracted' or perhaps 'dialectical ruin', a melancholy space of contradictory meaning, simultaneously remembering and forgetting itself.

The Sydenham Palace was not only a vast collection of static displays of historical space. It had restaurants and tearooms, an exhibitor's department where consumer goods could be purchased, it hosted all kinds of events including dog-shows and a forty-thousand strong annual co-op meeting. Most significantly, it played a massive role in the musical life of London. The Sydenham Palace was the scene of not only some of the most incredible musical spectacles of the age, but would also play host to one of the most significant moments in modern musical culture. Besides the musical tuition in the art school, two public musical venues were set up within the palace. In amongst the courts, a small concert room was created for chamber music. This was one of the main venues in London at which touring virtuosi would perform recitals; great names such as Leopold Godowsky, Federico Busoni and Moriz Rosenthal all performed there, but more significantly it was also the space in which many continental composers – such as Schubert, Schumann and Brahms – were first popularised in the UK. The seemingly unchanging pantheon of art-music that we are now familiar with was formed and distilled at Sydenham.[42] Most prominently however, at the west end of the main transept a massive auditorium was created, the biggest yet built by a huge margin. This space became famous for hosting the triennial Handel Festival, where choirs and musicians from all over the country would travel to London to perform a number of concerts over the course of a weekend. The scale of these events is incredible – the massed orchestra numbered seven hundred, the choir three thousand, performing to audiences of over twenty thousand people. These festivals presented great problems to the organisers; the space could effortlessly accommodate vast numbers of people, but there were terrible problems with acoustics; a ferro-vitreous palace is a highly reverberant space, and the earliest concerts would have been spectacles of huge but somewhat indistinct noise. Various devices were introduced to muffle the acoustics, and by all accounts they greatly improved the experience.[43]

We mentioned the role of the Hyde Park Palace in the rise and dissemination of photography; the Sydenham Palace was also the

The concert hall at the Crystal Palace

site of a number of highly significant developments in media technology. It was at the Handel Festival of 1888 that the Edison Gramophone Company would make the first ever piece of recorded music, during a gigantic performance of Handel's Moses & Aaron.[44] The wax cylinder upon which it was recorded still exists, and digital recordings have been made of it.[45] It bears description, both as a comparison to the role that the Hyde Park Palace played in early photography, but also in terms of ways in which we evoke and describe temporally distant objects, expanding the notion of the abstracted ruin that we have introduced. The most prominent aspect of the recording is the sounds of the dust, scratches and overall decay of the wax medium upon which it was recorded. The orchestra and chorus are audible, but in greatly transfigured forms; the orchestra is an indistinct rumble, all the instruments coalesced into a singly grainy sound, while the choir drifts in and out of audibility, their words indiscernible, a barely existing melody sometimes appearing out of the crackling noise of the cylinder's disintegration. This particular semi-disintegrated quality is an analogy of the process of memory itself; the sounds are invariably incomplete, drifting

37

in and out of intelligibility and adrift from any solid ground that would anchor them to a specific sonic fact. The resonance is two-fold; on the one hand this drifting, fragmented quality of memory is analogous to the spatial logic that was described before of incomplete spaces adrift in an almost immaterial fog, but it also speaks to us about our relationship to objects that are lost in their original state – the architecture thus far discussed is non-existent, accessible to us only as drawings, photographs, writings and memories, and in this case as distant sounds. There are very specific lessons to be drawn out here; all architecture, here under-stood perhaps as a Victorian architect might do as the 'art' of the building, that part of it which is insufficiently explained by an analysis of function, that which is concerned with 'meaning' – all architecture is in some way an archive, an immaterial statement preserved in a solid form, or a document of sorts. Both of the Crystal Palaces were statements that in a strong sense related to knowledge – they were collections, filled with objects to know and be remembered. But what is the nature of the condition whereby the only access to these moments of architecture is through the trace, through archive? What is being described in these cases? We should return to the term 'spectrality' here. As previously mentioned, 'spectrality' is Derrida's word for the condition of mediated presence; the ghostliness of repetition through recording, as described by Jameson: 'This is the other face of modern or we might say postmodern virtuality, a daily spectrality that undermines the present and the real without any longer attracting any attention at all'.[46]

We only have access to the Crystal Palaces through ghostly means; the abstracted ruin that we previously discussed must now be understood as being ghostly in another register. Indeed; the Crystal Palace seems, in a way, to have attracted spectral media; John Logie Baird, one of the inventors of television, moved his studios into the Crystal Palace in 1933. Why is this significant? Well; on the one hand, the more we delve into the inherently vanishing nature of the Crystal Palaces, the more their ephemerality is set in contrast to the monumentality that is the source of much of the normal power of architecture. Not only this, but we are also beginning to conceptually frame a certain notion of architecture that is perhaps unique; a fragile modernity; a dream-like, ghostly, abstracted ruin. We will continue to trace this form as we continue through the study.

If we wished to set up a simple dichotomy between the contemporary meaning of the two palaces then we might say that the Hyde Park Palace signified temporariness, while the Sydenham Palace signified permanence. Needless to say, this is deeply reductive, and perhaps we might complicate matters a little thus: The Hyde Park Palace was a building tending towards a 'pure' system, which nevertheless shied away from the implications of its own logic, while the Sydenham Palace was a building in which two very different logics were attempting to operate at once. For while the Sydenham Palace was intended to be as permanent as any massive masonry edifice, and while it had been redesigned to be a work of 'architecture', the logic of prefabrication and efficiency still permeated its very fabric. The accelerated decrepitude that results, which we shall have opportunity to further explore later, is something that will always haunt the architecture of systems, of temporariness and flexibility.

This temporariness affects how the buildings compare in history. The Great Exhibition, although obviously not as monolithically magnificent as is commonly believed, was spared an ignominious fate by its very ephemerality. On the one hand the Sydenham Palace had a much easier task to fulfil, seeing as it would not be the location of any massive festivals on the scale of its predecessor – the attempt to repeat the feat of the Great Exhibition in a brand new building in 1862 just months after the death of Prince Albert was, although not pathetic, still nowhere near as successful both in terms of money and in cultural resonances.[47] But on the other hand, the Sydenham Palace had to maintain public interest over a much longer period of time – and sustaining such a plateau of activity was in many ways a more difficult proposition.

The Crystal Palace as a romantic ruin, after the partial fire of 1866

The decline of the Sydenham Palace was a slow one. The palace was popular enough in the late 1850s and the 1860s, but by the 1870s visitor numbers had drastically reduced. The financial situation was poor; partly as a result of Paxton spending vast amounts of the initial capital of the Crystal Palace Company on the fountains; partly because Christian groups managed to have the palace closed on Sundays; partly through general mismanagement; and also because gradually the social mix of visitors to the palace narrowed to effectively include only the petit-bourgeoisie.[48] The 1870s saw a number of impassioned pleas to save the institution, which was considered to have lost sight of its noble ideals and was sinking into a pit of moral inequity:

> The establishment is at present a financial wreck. The
> building and the grounds are, to a grievous extent, in a state
> of material wreck [...] a visit by any one who remembers what
> the place once was [goes] some way to justify the statement
> that it is also in a state of moral wreck [...] Were the worst to
> come, were this ennobling institution to become really
> degraded, of which there appear sad, sad, premonitory
> symptoms, it would not only fail, but sink immeasurably
> below failure.[49]

Eventually, by 1911 the palace was bringing in so little money
and was in such a poor physical state that the palace and the
grounds were put up for auction. Although it was seen as being
a 'white elephant', its symbolic value to the nation meant that the
government made the purchase, and so the palace lurched on
throughout the next few decades as a public institution. By this
time the emphasis on 'Empire' that had always been one of the
unpleasant sides to the entire exhibition culture was now one of
the defining characteristics of the building; the park was the
location for the 1911 Empire Exhibition, before becoming home
to the Imperial War Museum for a number of years after the First
World War, with cannons mounted in the aisles and barrage
balloons moored in the transept. The quality of the entertainment dropped, the money kept disappearing into upkeep, so
that by the end of its life it was in such a sorry state that commentators were moved to make such sentimental descriptions as this,
from CF Bell-Knight's book on the palace;

> I recall a visit to the Crystal Palace during a summer in the
> mid 1930's; it presented a most woe-begone picture, peeling
> and sun blistered paintwork, the glass grimy, ironwork
> encrusted with rust and stonework suffering from erosion.

Overall was a film of black dust that seemed to invade everywhere, caused by the cinder ash which arose in clouds from the racing track. The fountains had ceased to function, possibly an economy drive, newspaper and wrappings floated disconsolately upon the oily waters of the lakes and pools. The outbuildings had fallen into disrepair, it was hazardous to negotiate the weed infested and cracked flights of steps and terraces. The grottos were literally refuse bins and fouled by urine and excreta. The shrubs were grossly overgrown and the borders unkempt...

That visit, which was my last before its final destruction, made such a lasting impression upon me that I can vividly conjure it up to this day. It really was a sad and sorry sight – as if the old palace was about to give up the ghost (as indeed it did not very long after) – but at least it went out in a final 'blaze of glory'.[50]

Eventually the Sydenham Palace burnt to the ground on the 30th November 1936. The death of the palace is often interpreted to be a highly symbolic one; within days of the conflagration German troops had landed in Spain, and Europe was about to be rent asunder all over again. Viewed in hindsight, it was easy to see the destruction of the palace as a portent of greater destruction, but it also marked the end of an era of Britain's 'greatness'; within years the empire would be all but gone and the UK would have to get used to playing its subservient global role in the new geopolitical order of the cold war.

But what of the Sydenham Palace now? One characteristic of a ferro-vitreous structure is that it doesn't ruin in the accepted aesthetic fashion. A masonry building has an entire aesthetic already developed for it to decay into, whereas an iron building, with its shards of glass and rust, is of a different visual order; rather than a ruin, a dead iron & glass palace has a skeleton. This lack of picturesque qualities, this hint of corporeality might perhaps explain why there are no 'stabilised ruins' made from iron & glass buildings; indeed, there are no direct traces of the actual palace at Sydenham today. The much-vaunted ephemerality of the construction has had its final triumph – there is no ruined palace on the site, but there is a massive disappearance, made tangible by the secondary objects left behind. At Sydenham this is clear from not only the masonry walls and staircases behind which the palace stood, which have indeed become little ruins, but from the expanses of blank space which used to feature in secondary roles to the dominance of the palace; these spaces are strange, subservient to something no longer there, playing second fiddle to an absence. The grand axiality of the space is another defining characteristic; broad avenues and promenades stretch out from the footprint of the palace, although they have nothing to lead up to apart from some scrubland. These blank spaces and pathways are decidedly empty; with no destination to draw people en masse, those who are present are dwarfed by the grandeur of the spatial arrangement, of which the sense of being in a space that was built for something that is no longer achievable is tangible. This particular sense is acutely melancholy – it hits straight at the centre of the logic of progress that was so important to the culture of exhibitions in the first place; instead of culture straining at the edges of the spaces which they use, pushing them out and forth, there is the sense of decline. Despite lacking the ruined artefact, what we have here, like the spaces of the Roman Forum being used as limekilns during the middle ages, is a vessel built to accommodate a grand purpose whose contemporary inhabitants are no longer capable of filling its empty space.

The Albert Palace

There is a definite historical hierarchy in the story of the early international exhibitions, with a trinity of the most significant. The 1851 London, 1889 Paris and the 1893 Chicago exhibitions are all well known and well documented, each with a specific historical character. 1851 was the original, 1889 the apotheosis of the cultural form, and 1893 is fondly remembered in the USA, but is also significant as a repudiation of the modern industrial architectural language that had been the style for the previous exhibitions. Less significant, but still famous are some other exhibitions. London in 1862 is the 'forgotten' exhibition, overshadowed by both the memory of the 1851 exhibition, but also the death of Prince Albert a couple of months beforehand. Paris in 1900 was the *Art Nouveau* exhibition, remembered for the ever so brief hegemony of the *Jugendstil* movement and for being the end of the iron & glass era and the beginning of the pavilion system, with each participating country building their own exhibit. The Paris Exposition of 1937, thoroughly overshadowed by the impending war, was notable for the absence of the USA, for Picasso's *Guernica,* and for the grim sight of the reactionary neo-classical German and Soviet pavilions facing off against each other in front of the Eiffel Tower.

But at another level of historical significance below that, the late 19th century saw the construction of a great number of less well remembered ferro-vitreous buildings, a great many exhibitions, a great many displays, a great number of spectacular failures. The 1873 Vienna Exhibition was an economic catastrophe, while the 1879 Australian Exhibition building burned to the ground in suspicious circumstances (the convict files had been stored there). The period around the 1880s saw perhaps the greatest number of international exhibitions than any other decade,[51] and a greater level of ferro-vitreous building than at any other time; [52] a flurry of activity that we might as well call iron & glass fever, fuelled by optimism, a taste for symbols of 'progress', as well as the patronising notion of social 'improvement', with all the over-compensated worries it entails.

Of all the buildings of this period, perhaps the most extreme case of failure and disappearance was a building called the Albert Palace (1885-94). This massive ferro-vitreous edifice once stood at the edge of Battersea Park, near the River Thames in London. But unlike the Crystal Palaces, which, misunderstood as they may be, have their proud position in the history of architectural culture, very few people alive have ever heard of the Albert Palace, and it merits no more than a passing mention in any history. One of the main reasons for this is that the building had a very short lifespan of less than ten years, but beyond this fleeting presence the building suffered a further ignominy, a historical disappearance that is nearly total. Very few records of the Albert Palace's existence survive – there appear to be no extant photographs, for example. This position of almost total non-existence contrasts rather significantly with the stories told previously of the two Crystal Palaces, of which huge amounts of documentary evidence still exist. The story of the Albert Palace should be seen as tending towards a limit condition of disappearance, an object that almost never existed in the very first place. Beyond that, its story is rather pitiful: an architectural tale of optimism, failure and melancholy.

One of the popular suggestions made for the future of the Crystal Palace after it was dismantled in Hyde Park was that it could be transported to and erected in Battersea Park, which had been recently set out next to the river at the edge of London, at that point growing rapidly along with the expansion of the railways. This was the preferred option of both Prince Albert and Sir Henry Cole, although as we have seen, Paxton's entrepreneurial skills allowed him to re-erect the Crystal Palace at Sydenham. It seems that the Prince Consort's idea was strong enough that nearly thirty years after his death it would be brought to fruition, and in his honour. The Albert Exhibition Palace Company was formed by Albert Grant, and later run by Sir Robert Walter Carden MP and Sir Edward Lee, an entrepreneur who had experience of running the education department at the Sydenham Palace, in an example of that peculiar system of Victorian philanthropic 'good works'.[53] Like the Sydenham Palace, the erection of this new building violated the architectural law of site-specificity – an already built palace was purchased, in this case the winter garden that had been constructed for the Dublin International Exhibition of 1865 (which Sir Edward Lee had been involved in managing), which was dismantled and shipped over the Irish Sea, to be reassembled as 'a sort of gigantic Chinese puzzle'.[54] The building purchased was, as with many of the ferro-vitreous buildings of the time, based upon a somewhat ecclesiastical arrangement; an arched nave flanked by galleries, in this case with the rather interesting touch of having webbed 'flying buttresses' springing from the roof which took the lateral load of the vault, and which on the exterior presented an attractively sinuous structural detail.[55] Although less than half the size of the Crystal Palace, it was still a massive space, 473ft long, 83ft wide and with a 60ft high vault.[56] In Dublin it had been attached to a large masonry building, creating a strange version of the 'hybrid construction'; the glass palace was fully displayed on three sides. Because of its abutment, the structure had been designed with insufficient lateral stability to stand on its own.[57] The remains of the recently demolished Law Courts at Westminster were purchased in order to create a masonry building to run along one façade, providing structural stability, extra space, and a 'proper' façade to face neighbouring buildings to the south.[58]

It is worth discussing the programme of the new Albert Palace as another example of an attempt to build a permanent ferro-vitreous 'People's Palace'. The main exhibition space was

The Albert Palace, Alfred Gresham Jones, 1885

described as a 'noble and lofty central hall' flanked by 'handsome galleries' running the entire length of the building, and in which were to be collected sculptures and other exhibits. In the ground floor of the masonry structure there were a number of rooms for entertainment, including a 'commodious tea room', a 'noble and lofty saloon' and a billiard room, as well as private dining rooms. On the upper level of the masonry structure there was a picture gallery, in which there were displays of fine art, although it would seem from the catalogue that it was not of any significant quality.[59] Half way along the central hall there was a semi-circular transept, described as a 'spacious orchestra', which was to be used for promenade concerts, and at one end of the building was the *'Connaught Hall'*, a specialised concert venue in the same mode as the Handel Orchestra at the Sydenham Palace, although not quite of the same ridiculous scale. In this space was installed one of the largest organs in the world, known as the 'Holmes Organ'.[60] The collection of spaces seems to have been lacking in the specifically commercial uses that by that point had overwhelmed the Sydenham Palace; apart from food and drink it does not seem that the building offered much in the way of consumables; it was less of a department store and more of a multimedia entertainment centre.

The Connaught Hall at the Albert Palace, 1885

After the transfer of the building to London in 1883, construction work was essentially finished by the end of 1884, with a view to opening the building in the summer of 1885. There was some anticipation for the opening of the building, but of a much smaller scale than that which attended the Crystal Palaces.

Architectural trade magazines such as *The Builder* visited the building as it was being constructed and reported upon its progress,[61] while local newspapers in the Battersea area followed it with interest, but this was not major news – there would be no royalty at the opening, and it would not be hosting any fantastic exhibitions on a national, let alone international scale. It was seen very much to be a permanent facility for locals and Londoners, one for which there was thought to be ample demand:

> Seeing that the "Palace" is situated in the midst of a large population, and that it is easily approachable from all parts of London by three railways and by tramways, as well as by steamboats in the summer, it ought to be a success, and no doubt will be, if well managed.[62]

The Sydenham Palace, at the centre of musical life in the London area, was a great influence on the proprietors of the Albert Palace, and music was seen to be one of the principle activities of the building. A.J. Caldicott, a lecturer of composition at the Royal College of Music (one of the Albertopolis institutions), was appointed as musical director, with a view to holding regular concerts and making the Albert Palace an important part of the musical life of the city. Caldicott orchestrated an ode by W.A. Barrett for the opening of the palace, a poem and composition which would seem to be lost, although the *Musical World's* description of the ode gives us a taste of the expectations of the building:

> In his poem, Mr Barrett contrasts the joyous strains of peace with the harsh notes of war; invokes a blessing on industry; makes grateful reference to the labours of the late Prince Consort, and ends by calling upon Music to lend its charm to an occasion full of hope and gladness.[63]

The Albert Palace opened on the 6th June 1885, and in another example of the potential for iron & glass to act as a portent, *The Builder* reported the event thus:

> The Albert Palace, Battersea Park, was opened on Saturday last, under very depressing circumstances so far as the weather was concerned. Nevertheless, the proceedings of the day augured well for the future of the Palace.[64]

It would seem to have been a most miserably wet day, although the organisers managed to put on a fireworks display afterwards.[65] This glumness of scene didn't affect the professed enthusiasm for the venture though; by all accounts the idea of a palace of culture set next to the pleasantries of the park was bound to be a success, the two reciprocally complementing each other's attractions.

As early as the end of that summer, however, the original administration of the company had collapsed; it would seem that not only had all involved overestimated the public demand for a building of such refined offerings of culture, but also that nobody was willing to input the capital required for the building's upkeep. Later, an obviously embittered Sir Edward Lee would describe the building as being like 'a birth-strangled babe', painting a very different picture to the optimists at the opening:

> It is a fact, nevertheless, that there was not as much money expended in furnishing and embellishing the entire Palace and grounds as the Crystal Palace Company spent on the production of the Alhambra Court alone [...] the whole stock-in-trade of permanent attractions consisted of a magnificent organ, a sprinkling of statuary, and a tolerably extensive collection of mediocre pictures.[66]

The struggling building was taken over by a Mr William Holland, who steered the palace away from notions of fine arts and betterment to turn it into something else entirely – an iron & glass 'music hall'. Over the next two years until 1888 the palace would host exhibitions such as 'The Pigmies or Dwarf Earth-Men'; 'Commodore Foote & Sister – The smallest, best educated, best looking, and most perfectly formed little people in the

The 'spacious orchestra' in the Albert Palace transept, 1885

World'; even Buffalo Bill Cody would appear.[67] But even this rather crass level of entertainment could not reverse the fortunes of the palace, and by the end of 1888 it had closed its doors permanently.

Over the next four years the building slowly decayed, with sparrows nesting in the organ, the glass palace reduced to the giant skeleton of some beached leviathan.[68] This, rather than the monumental ruin, is the aesthetic of fallen iron & glass: rather than a vision of humanity's transience as represented by broken columns and fragmented statuary, we have an object that is directly redolent of a corpse. At an auction in 1892 no bids at all were made for the building, and there was no attempt to save it made by the government.[69] However by this time a movement had begun in the local area to attempt a rescue of the building. In an example of an engaged politics that might seem utterly alien to the culture of the current day, a number of public meetings were held over the course of the year, committees formed, parliamentarians lobbied, speeches made and votes taken. There was a strong urge to restore the building with plenty of local support, but debates went on about to what purpose the building could be put, how much it would cost, and who should pay – private investors, the local council of Battersea or the County Council of London. It was decided that the building would make an excellent winter garden extension to Battersea Park, with the 'Connaught Hall' being made available for concerts and political meetings; essentially a reduced version of the programme as it had originally been set out. It was said that 'it would be a sin and a scandal if the building were not secured for the people of Battersea'.[70] By October, the movement (referred to in the press as 'Albert Palace for the People') had gathered pace, the meetings were attracting crowds of people who came to listen to rousing speeches such as that of Mr John Burns, independent MP for Battersea and one of the first working class members of the British parliament (Battersea once had a reputation as a most radical part of London, and would become home to communist councillors and the first black mayor in Britain), reported by *The South-Western Star* thus:

> They wanted the Albert Palace because it would be a sin and a shame to pull such a building down when they would get hardly £50 for the materials of which it was composed. It ought to be a London suburban palace approximating as closely as possible the to the ideal of Walter Besant – a people's palace in the best and truest sense of the word (cheers).[71]

This over-riding concern for the building being purchased on behalf of 'the People' was further stressed by the words of Mr. Percy M. Thornton, MP for Clapham, who said, to round applause, 'the object we all here desire is the happiness of the people, and in their interest and the interest of the neigh-bourhood I have given my adherence to the scheme for acquiring the Albert Palace for the neighbourhood'.[72] By the end of the month the £20,000 for the acquisition of the palace had seemingly been raised with the promise of £10,000 from John Passmore Edwards, the legendary media mogul and philan-thropist who had recently begun building the numerous libraries and other public works that he would later be remembered for.[73] For the second time in the life of the palace there was great optimism for the future, and by the end of 1892 it was comfortably thought that the palace would soon be acquired and transformed into a winter garden.

There was no mention of the Albert Palace in the press throughout 1893, but then in January 1894 the following exchange occurred in Parliament;

> Mr Shaw Lefevre: I have received information from the hon. member for Battersea (Mr. Burns.) that he has been compelled

to abandon the scheme for the purchase of the Albert Palace, and for transferring it to the London County Council as a place of public recreation. In these circumstances I deem it my duty to realise the property as soon as possible. The building will, therefore, be removed and the site used for building purposes.[74]

It would seem that the London County Council were only prepared to give their portion of the money for the purchase of the palace if they were not also required to pay for its upkeep. In light of this stalemate, and despite the efforts of John Burns, there was nothing that could be done.

Finally, on June the 2nd, 1894 *The South Western Star* featured an article entitled 'Adieu to the Albert Palace: A Melancholy Scene'; a short piece that is surely a paradigmatic example of architectural melancholy, an example of Victorian sentimentalism at its worst and most mawkish, but at the same time a text which speaks volumes about architecture and its role as a repository of memory. The main passage of the piece is a reminiscence, the journalist standing within the Palace and running through the events that occurred there:

It seems but yesterday that we were called upon to assist at the festivities which marked the formal inauguration of the "Albert Palace of Science and Art," and to listen to speeches of much eloquence in which members of Parliament and others told us how much the new institution was going to do for the intellectual and moral elevation of Battersea.[75]

The journalist goes on to mention 'the Viennese Ladies' Orchestra', fetes, political meetings, 'fancy dress balls concerning which the less said the better', 'Mexican Joe and his more or less wild Indians', as well as a number of other anecdotes. All are fragmentary, partial memories structured around the skeleton of the broken palace in which he stands:

Where are those barties *(sic)* now? One might as well inquire as to the where-abouts of *les nuges d'autun. (sic)* They have vanished into *Ewigkeit,* and soon there will be no building in which their ghosts can walk. Nothing save memory will remain.

This rather pretentious passage begins to involve a particular set of tropes concerning memory and architecture; firstly the language of clouds – as discussed with regard to the Sydenham Palace and sound, a common metaphor for the decay of memory is that of the fog, the cloud, dust and ash, in the way that they occlude and transfigure an object. Next comes the sense of irretrievability of the impending loss, a nothingness that will last for eternity, before the writer introduces the language of ghostliness. Cultures of haunting are inextricably tied into notions of space and temporality, and in this case we have an example of the haunting understood as the trace of the event that is spatially coexistent but temporally distant. The fact that the impending absence of the palace means an end to the haunting is also significant – according to the journalist, the memories he is recounting absolutely depend upon the space in which they occurred; the memories themselves are archived there. If the Albert Palace vanishes, there is nothing left to remember, and so we are left with the most pitiful scene, the rain falling on the last day of its life as it rained on the day of its opening.

...the last scene of all was of a most depressing character. Even the heavens wept to gaze upon such a scene, for as soon as the auctioneer had taken up his position in front of the dismantled stage a heavy shower of natural tears descended, and very soon they were trickling down the pillars of the Palace and forming little pools beneath the feet of the hard hearted men, gathered as ravens to the carcase.

There was nothing to disturb the monotony – all around was damp and gloomy, the associations were too melancholy, and folding his note-book the South-Western Star man glided silently away, leaving the Albert Palace of Science and Art, "A thing o-er which the raven flapped her fun'ral wing.

After the auction the building was demolished; the organ was purchased and removed to Fort Augustus Abbey at the end of Loch Ness in Scotland, where it stood until the abbey was converted into luxury flats a few years ago – the fate of the organ is unclear.[76] The iron structure of the palace was purchased with a view to re-erecting it as part of the Earl's Court Exhibition centre, but it was found to be too heavy for the ground, and sold on for scrap, thus finally ending the physical existence of the building, even in a reconstituted, fragmented or trace-like state.[77] Within a few years the land upon which it stood had been purchased by property developers, who proceeded to build two blocks of 'mansions' – that peculiar London typology of luxury flats of the late Victorian and early Edwardian period. The block facing the park goes by the name of the 'Albert Palace Mansions', which is the only trace of the building of any kind left there whatsoever, a fittingly immaterial one.

So what is the significance of the Albert Palace and its tale of woe? On the one hand it is a simple story of a failed business venture – it would seem that those involved saw the lack of investment in the building as the main reason for its failure, a familiar story when it comes to architecture. But it is not as simple as that – most, if not all of the exhibition buildings made permanent were business failures – the Crystal Palace Company lasted longer than most, but the Sydenham Palace haemorrhaged money from the very beginning, while other London buildings such as the People's Palace in Mile End (1892-1931), The Royal Aquarium in Westminster (1876-1903) and the Alexandra Palace on Muswell Hill (1873-) all lurched from financial failure to financial failure. This is partially due to any new technology being prone to all kinds of unforeseen problems and snags, a troublesome side to new-ness that somewhat clouds its vanguard glory, and a problem that has dogged all high-technology architecture since. As mentioned before, it is often more important to signify than to be, and in this case the statement refers to the often counterintuitive decisions that must be taken to implement a new technology. That this was an issue is testified to by the reluctance of the council to pay for the maintenance, but in the wider context, even at the time there was a sense that there was something particularly amiss about iron & glass:

> The struggle for existence is difficult to the Albert Palace, and has proved impossible for the Alexandra Palace; it has given it up altogether. Some fate, or perhaps some occult law of nature, works against them. Glass, as we know, is an excellent non-conductor of heat; it is possible that it is also a non-conductor of coin & prosperity.[78]

Hyperbole aside, it is fascinating to see the language of fate being used to talk about an architectural mode. With all the portents that we have seen, we can say that there is a hint of the tragic about iron & glass. Combined with the technological-romanticism of their aesthetics, we already have a strong case for their being considered 'melancholy' architecture. But we should not stop there. It would be naïve to look purely at maintenance as the source of the failures [79] – a small number of buildings in iron & glass have survived till the present day, after all. Any reckoning with the reasons for the failures of the palaces has to focus upon the social functions and cultural attitudes embedded in these buildings. Both the Sydenham Palace and the Albert Palace started out as facilities of lofty, if patronising ideals:

providing culture to the 'masses', a contradictory impulse born of genuine concern, but also of the imperative to protect the existing social order from any radical change coming from below: as Benjamin notes – 'Side by side with the overt position of philanthropy, the bourgeoisie has always maintained the covert position of class struggle'.[80] In the complicated case of the Albert Palace however, a battle was fought by a radical politician for the purchase of the building explicitly on behalf of the local working classes, a welcome if futile change from the politics of condescension. That these houses of culture never managed to pay for themselves is partly due to some of the massive social changes going on at the time; the spectacular culture that the Great Exhibition was the harbinger of would develop so rapidly that it would quickly bring on the obsolescence of such concentrated spaces of educational entertainment. But we should go further again; there is yet more to the failure of the palaces. The ferro-vitreous buildings were among the biggest enclosed spaces ever created at that time, and as we have seen with spaces like the Handel Orchestra, the size of event that needed to take place in order to fill the space could be absolutely massive. To sustain that level of interest was not only a near impossible task but, as previously described, the self-perpetuating melancholy feeling of the space that is far too large for whatever takes place inside it must already have been palpable, even before their disappearance. In the case of the Albert Palace, that they had not the money to adequately fill the building from the very beginning must have given the whole exhibition hall a tangible sense of inadequacy. The ability to build the space outstripped the ability to fill it.

But the other important aspect of the Albert Palace's story is in its relationship with disappearance. Like the Crystal Palaces, the only access we have to the Albert Palace is mediated through images and verbal descriptions. But unlike these famous buildings, the Albert Palace left almost no trace whatsoever, with no extant photographs, a lifespan so short that it appeared on hardly any maps, and only a handful of documents still left that make any reference to it whatsoever. In fact, we could say that its history tends towards total disappearance, a limit condition whereby all physical, archived evidence of an event is destroyed, thus effectively denying it the very possibility of ever being encountered. It goes without saying that even in our era of hyper-documentation, our archive is nothing but a tiny light in an ocean of darkness. Inasmuch as the dead will always outnumber the living, so that which is forgotten will always overwhelm that which is remembered. As time passes, if there is no document within our archive to testify to an event or an object, then it didn't happen – to us at this time, the Albert Palace very nearly didn't exist at all.

In this way the Albert Palace becomes a figure for us of the limit-condition of architectural ephemerality, of architectural spectrality, of ghostliness. The fleetingly short life of the building puts into question the very relationship between space and archive – where the building is normally a guarantor of memory, here it too becomes fragment and dream; the permanent is revealed in its own transience. The spectral is the figure of this *unheimlich* quality to everyday temporality, a representative of moments of presence that are distant in time, a trope that describes the nagging residual gaps at the heart of reality. In architecture *qua* archive, this phenomenal spectrality becomes concrete. It is a petrification of memory, a setting in stone that corresponds to the tendency of memory itself to decay. If 'the structure of the archive is spectral'[81], then a building such as the Albert Palace is in its own way a ghost, haunting our archive at the very edge of disappearance.

The 'ruin' as we normally understand it is tied into this logic of monumentality; of physical trace, of 'archive', even in its most transient state. However, the logic of the ruin is already at work in the iron & glass palaces, even when they are at their most complete. These 'abstract ruins' inherently suggest ephemerality, we can see this not only in the poetic language they inspired, but also in the political and cultural attitudes held towards them. We cannot speak of a necessary link between the spatial dematerialisation of the palaces and their failure, but by the end of this study it will be difficult to merely attribute it to coincidence, especially when we consider later attempts to move towards a demonumentalised architectural culture. The palaces are already in the process of forgetting themselves, yet architecture is relied upon for its memorial function: 'Objects made of glass have no 'aura.' says Benjamin.[82] We will soon note how this lack of aura has been interpreted as a culturally radical condition.

Modernity and the Engineer Genius

Hidden Iron and Glass : The Machinery Building at the World's
Columbian Exposition, Robert Swain Peabody, 1893

In the first section of the book we told the story of a number of
individual buildings, drawing lessons from their histories. The
second section will approach a number of recent movements in
architectural culture that have led up to the current impasse. The
concepts sharpened by the study of the iron & glass buildings
will provide us with tools with which to evaluate the movements
studied; we will see how the iron & glass buildings act as a
paradigm, and as neglected precedents of the current situation.
Before this, however, we will need to consider the immediate
impact of ferro-vitreous architecture on the late 19th and early
20th centuries.

    Although contemporaries were well aware of the revolu-
tionary nature of the developments in iron construction of the
mid-19th century, the forced distinction between architect and

engineer was maintained all the way up until the early 20th century, as the intellectual and aesthetic problems of eclecticism continued unresolved. In Britain the Gothic revival was basically unaffected by the rationalist contention that iron & glass buildings were the new cathedrals, structurally reduced and materially efficient, and even Joseph Paxton was to take on further architectural projects in a revivalist style.[83] In 1861 he made an (unbuilt) design for his largest glass palace yet, for Saint Cloud in France, but would not return to the mode again before his death in 1873.[84] The new technology was implemented regularly, but previous aesthetic systems remained at the surface.

The period of iron & glass engineering was gradually brought to a close with the introduction of two yet-newer materials: steel and reinforced concrete. The development of the Bessemer process of steel making in 1855 rapidly reduced the cost of the material, and by the end of the century it had superseded wrought iron as the primary metallic construction material. The fact that structural metal was now generally 'rolled' in more-or-less arbitrary lengths of constant section meant that the aesthetic qualities of cast iron and its ability to be detailed were generally lost; future steel frames would be mostly gridded collections of I-beams, rarely exposed to the gaze. Apart from the art-nouveau explosion at the turn of the century, the use of iron was on the decline, meaning that by the middle of the 20th century the only cast-iron objects in architecture were things like radiators, lamp-posts, or Sir Giles Gilbert-Scott's iconic K6 telephone kiosks, which perhaps we can romantically and not a little ironically see as the last remaining relatives of the ferro-vitreous palaces; the birds to their dinosaurs. By the turn of the century ferrous construction had become relatively common, thus somewhat deadening its marvellous quality, but at the same time the iron & glass palaces had never managed to be properly accepted as genuine architectural forms, and historicism was still the dominant mode – masonry facades were most common when building a steel-framed building, as seen in the development of the skyscraper typology in the USA. The skyscraper represents another cultural change – the winter gardens were long and relatively low buildings, but towards the end of the 19th century there was great upward pressure on building forms, and perhaps signified by the Eiffel Tower, height was the new boundary to be stretched.

But ferro-concrete was a technological shift with much greater significance. Concrete had been in use since at least Roman times (the Pantheon being a great example), but the development of reinforced concrete in the 1870s was its own revolution in architecture. By combining the tensile strength of metal with the compressive strength of concrete a new wonder material was born that was capable both of the structural gymnastics that the 19th century engineer geniuses had pioneered, but at the same time could be moulded into almost any shape, as massive or as weightless as could be wished. This plasticity would be of great importance to the modernists, giving sculptural and expressive possibilities that metal could not. Architects such as Auguste Perret could work with the revolutionary material without necessarily abandoning the lessons of their Beaux-Arts training, and the solidity of concrete made it more appropriate to play a part in a monumental city ensemble.

Some radical groups would still make appeals to the all-glass aesthetic; for instance the more expressive wing of the Deutsche Werkbund looked to the mystical and fantastic qualities of glass as a material, but their efforts would eventually flow into the stream of the Bauhaus modernism pioneered by Gropius et al. Although glass would still play a vital role in the European modernist aesthetic, it would not be in the 'crystal' sense of the winter gardens and glass palaces.

But were there descendents of the iron & glass palaces? What happened to the architecture of the future when, at the end of the 19th century; 'these buildings vanished from the mental horizon like a fata morgana, like a shimmering soap bubble that could not survive the forces of the times and burst into tiny pieces'?[85] As the exhibition palaces and winter gardens went into decline and disappeared, the engineer's art would still govern the construction of railway stations, factories, bridges and infra-structure, slowly becoming so familiar in its ubiquity that it would be considered relatively commonplace. However these buildings would never achieve the phantasmagorical qualities that we have analysed, only hinting at the strangeness of the 'Palaces of the People'. Indeed, as we have noted, the later 19th century actually saw a retreat from the lightness and fragility of the iron & glass palaces, in favour of the massive eccentricities of eclecticism. But we *can* see aspects of the culture of consumption inaugurated at the Great Exhibition in the late 20th century super-markets with their endless brightly lit displays of consumable goods, and in their arrangements and structures, the shopping mall harks back to the covered arcades of the 19th century. As we will discuss later, a similar form of cultural building 'for the people' would appear around the late 20th century in the form of the super-museum, the 'supermarket of culture', while we can also see the sublime effects of such fantastic size and unadorned structures in sports stadiums, with their openly expressed cantilevers and massive crowded spaces. But despite these similarities, the palaces and winter gardens are unrepeatable events. The rise of spectacular capitalism, and its attendant media – cinema, recorded music, television etc – would make it impos-sible to hold singular, unified events displaying these cultures: the international exhibitions marked the end of the possibility of conceiving such a totality of culture.

But one of the most important qualities of the iron & glass palaces is, to use a cliché, the prismatic way that they reflect the cultures that created and used them. I have discussed how the elite's fears of revolution were a driving force in the creation of the palaces, and how the recurring concerns about education and betterment betray a deep and constant cultural anxiety regarding the vulnerability of the status-quo. However, at the very same time the palaces were symbols of progress and futurism, especially to radicals; in his *Garden Cities of Tomorrow,* the urban reformer Ebenezer Howard proposed large arcades or 'Crystal Palaces' accommodating shopping facilities and winter gardens as part of his dream.[86] Howard's attitude was somewhat unambitious, and when 'garden cities' actually began to be built, the arcades never materialised.

A more utopian view of the Crystal Palace can be found in Chernyshevsky's novel *What is to be Done?* In a celebrated passage the Sydenham Palace (which Chernyshevsky visited in 1859) appears to the heroine in a dream; functioning as a symbol of a peaceful socialist future brought about through rationalism and technology.[87] However, Dostoyevsky in *Notes from Underground* mocks Chernyshevsky and the Crystal Palace (which he visited in 1862), seeing it as a symbol of stifling modernity in which everything is calculated and freedom is impossible.[88] These two attitudes show Janus faces of modernity; on the one hand the promise of greater freedom through technology, on the other the crushing lack of freedom in an overly rational world. Both of these men used the Crystal Palace for its symbolic embodiment of modernity but as we've noted before, in the UK the implications of its modernity were both far more complex than these two extreme metaphors would suggest. In fact, its implications were also somewhat traumatic for the bourgeoisie that created it, as Marshall Berman noted; 'it might be argued that the unwillingness of the British bourgeoisie to accept and live with such a brilliant expression of its own modernity presaged its gradual loss of energy and imagination'.[89] This is an intriguing thesis; one that bears comparison to what we noted before about the relationship of the palaces to monumentality.

And against monumentality, weakness is, perhaps, one of the

defining characteristics of the palaces and their culture. From the very simple sense that compared to all architecture that had gone before the palaces looked as delicate as a spider's web, 'the most fairy-like production of Architectural Art that had yet been produced';[90] ethereal, almost completely transparent; to the worries before the Great Exhibition that the building would collapse at the first heavy wind; to the very word 'Crystal', with its connotations of the fragility of glass, to their susceptibility to fire and collapse; to their pathetic fights against commercial decline, we should stress the strong narratives of weakness that attend the culture of the iron & glass buildings.

We have already seen how some 19th century historians could simultaneously praise the engineering genius of the Crystal Palace and its aesthetic beauty while simultaneously asserting its inability to be considered as architecture. Similarly, differing modernist histories would ascribe varying and contradictory levels of influence to iron & glass. At one extreme was the purely formalist system originating in America, where Henry-Russell Hitchcock and the erstwhile fascist Philip Johnson would present *The International Style*.[91] This 1932 exhibition at New York's Museum of Modern Art would whitewash the radical politics of various European modernists into a clean style of white painted concrete. Hitchcock would always stress what he saw as the American influences upon European modernism, and when presenting another show at MOMA in 1937 called *Modern Architecture in England*, he would suggest that the Crystal Palace was, in a fine example of damnation by faint praise; 'a monument often hailed with pardonable exaggeration as the first modern building',[92] And that 'the line of development toward modern architecture through the bold and imaginative use of metal ended in 1851 in England'.[93] To him, the main predecessor of modernism in the UK was the Glasgow School of Art (1897-) by C.M. Mackintosh. This absolute masterpiece of a building does indeed presage a great number of later methods and approaches, as well as creating spatial effects that were unprecedented at the time. Historically considered however, it is a 'deep' building, full of reference and knowledge: it does not attempt to forge a new context against tradition, with the political implications that that might suggest. Instead we might think of it as a 'timeless' building, architecture *qua* architecture. It can only be the forerunner of a modernism stripped of its disjunctive qualities.

Central and Western Europe would be the developing ground of the somewhat oxymoronic 'modernist tradition', from the Bauhaus in Germany to Le Corbusier in France, and all the other peripheral figures who made up the avant-garde of the inter-war period. At this time as much as any other there were reams of architectural theories being published, but at this point they were produced with greater fervour, as radicals attempted to consolidate their positions through conceptual and historical exegesis. Le Corbusier was an acknowledged master; supplementing his not-particularly-prolific built oeuvre with frequent texts in which he put forward his theories of the problems to which his buildings were the solution. Amongst what we might call theorists of modernism, one task was common to all; the correction of the historical denigration of the engineer. Nearly all modernists were in agreement that 'the Machine Age' required an architecture that was capable of expressing the aspects of culture that were particular to it. One of the first tasks that needed to be accomplished was the rehabilitation of the engineer after the revivalist periods, while also protecting the engineer from the aestheticising tendencies within modernism.

Siegfried Giedion's book *Building in France, Building in Iron, Building in Ferro-Concrete* (1928) is one of the earliest modernist statements rehabilitating the 19th century engineer genius. It is the main source of Walter Benjamin's architectural speculations in *The Arcades Project*, and one of the first texts to properly proclaim Le Corbusier as the most important architect then currently working. Politically we can see it as falling into that particular attitude so very common to the modernist architect, a sort of technocratic quasi-socialism; very keen on the planned solution to social problems through state control, with little mention of re-organised means of production or redistribution of wealth. As part of the consolidation period of modernism, amid the attempts to normalize the chaos of a new language, Giedion posits his role to be as a kind of 'active historian': against the notion of closed-history, where 'The historian, unfortunately, has used the perspective of his occupation to give eternal legitimation to the past and thereby to kill the future, or at least to obstruct its development'. Giedion claims that, in a way that would have been of great interest to Benjamin, 'the historian's task appears to be the opposite: to extract from the vast complexity of the past those elements that will be the point of departure for the future'.[94] Specifically this would mean creating a new narrative for the 'constructor'; the 19th century engineer whose achievements, far from threatening the role of the architect as the academics would have it, would sweep academicism aside and point the way forward to a new freedom for all architects, creating a new synthesis of form and function that would go some way towards mending the modern psyche. This new narrative would not just demonstrate a method that architects should be following, but on the other hand it could defend modernism from critical attack by showing that, far from being unprecedented, 'the architecture we now describe as "new" is a legitimate part of an entire century of development'.[95]

Giedion focuses his polemic on industrial construction as it developed in France, and for some reason feels it important to denigrate English ferro-vitreous construction; he claims that the Crystal Palace demonstrated a 'fear of open space', and that 'the English, in fact, are less talented as constructors' when compared to French innovators like Labrouste.[96] Even over a decade later in his *Space, Time and Architecture*, he would complain that the Crystal Palace led to no new discoveries in the problem of iron vaulting, before somewhat grudgingly conceding that 'the possibilities dormant in modern industrial civilisation have never since, to my knowledge, been so clearly expressed'.[97] One of the reasons for this neglect is perhaps because Giedion's attention is most focused on demonstrating the development of the two greatest achievements of the 'constructor': the Galerie des Machines and the Eiffel Tower. To Giedion, 'The exhibition on 1889 is both the climax and – interpreted from the standpoint of knowledge – the conclusion of this development'[98.]In this he should be taken seriously.

It might be stating the obvious, but the Eiffel Tower is the most significant material product of the world exhibitions that still exists. Despite being as temporary as any other exhibition structure, despite the vociferous opposition to its very construction in the first place, and despite the frequent collapse of other attempts to make permanent structures out of the exhibitions, it still stands proudly over Paris. Two specific things mark it out from any other 19th century exhibition structure; one, it is an almost sublimely useless piece of architecture – it barely encloses any space at all. It functions almost purely as an icon, a symbol of itself and the city in which it stands, and in that way we might crudely say it functions like many a modern European monarchy; a pointless relic that nonetheless adds a sense of romance and brings in the tourists. It has also been ever-popular with suicides. The other thing that marks it out is its verticality – rather than being an enclosure over a large area of ground, it is mostly open structure. We can perhaps suggest that this allowed it to seem important long into the twentieth century, with the rise of the skyscraper as the technological limit of building. In fact; it was the tallest 'building' in the world for almost forty years after its construction.

But the Galerie des Machines didn't survive. Demolished in 1910, in what Giedion would quote famously as 'an act of artistic sadism', it is yet another building only accessible to us through

Limit of Iron & Glass : The Galerie des Machines at the Paris
Exposition, Ferdinand Dutert, 1889

archive material and a series of haunting photographs.[99] And like
the crystal palaces, it represents a weakness, a point of failure in
the functionalist narrative being created at this time. In the
century-long period between the first experiments in iron
construction and the Paris Exposition of 1889, the limits of
engineering were continually being pushed back, with bigger
spaces, wider spans, higher roofs. There were brand new architectural problems, often generated by the rapid urbanisation in
industrialised economies, and the accompanying infrastructural
developments, such as railways and other distribution networks.
The level of discovery at this period was such that it would have
been very difficult *not* to perceive a sense of limitless progress as
the boundaries of human structural achievement were regularly
and frequently refined. But it is very difficult to discover
something twice. The Crystal Palace was a massive test of the

abilities of manufacturing to produce a building of that size, that quickly, to the extent that to this day it is cited as being the largest area covered in the shortest time, ever.[100] This straining against limits that is the essence of the 'constructor' narrative reaches its apotheosis in the 1889 exhibition; the Eiffel Tower was the tallest structure in the world, almost doubling the height of the Washington Monument, and the Galerie des Machines, at 420m long and 115m wide, was the longest single space in the world, with the widest single span. While the humungous yet precise beauty of the Galerie's three-hinged arches perched *en point* in their brackets are still eulogised to this day, their seemingly precarious visual power being marked as a decisive break with concepts of monumentality, the building itself reveals some strange problems. During the exhibition the building was, as its name might suggest, filled with industrial machinery, and it was so large that an elevated railway was constructed to carry visitors from one end of the clattering sea of exhibits to the other. This problem marks a limit of another kind; with the two main buildings of 1889 the engineers uncovered another problem – what to do with all this space they'd created. The Eiffel Tower was effectively an industrial sculpture, with only the barest of programmes. The Galerie des Machines however, being an enclosed space, was thus undoubtedly a building, its vast interior a room, but a room of a scale never before seen: what could possibly fill this space again? Instead of (as was the case for the Crystal Palace) new engineering achievements being catalysed by programmatic demands, in 1889 the engineers set the challenge to human culture; we had been overtaken by our own abilities. The heroic reciprocity that defined ferro-vitreous building culture was now effectively at an end: this is how we should understand Giedion's statement about 'conclusion'.

We noted before about how the absence of the Crystal Palace from the park in Sydenham creates an uncanny sense of an over-provision of space, a variety of the sublime bearing with it a certain melancholy feeling that is related to, but not necessarily commensurate with, that of the ruin. We should understand the passing in 1889 of the ability of culture to give proper challenges to the 'constructors' as a similar condition. It is the initial moment of failure in functionalist narratives; this period of structural achievement caused a form of alienation, whereby human abilities were no longer capable of forcing structural discoveries. The only limits now were economic ones, and aestheticisation would always be attendant from then on, albeit always disavowed to a greater or lesser extent. We ought to concede that in some ways it is not particularly surprising that there was a shrinking back from the implications of the ferro-vitreous revolution. The relationship between architecture and its engineering has not only been shown to have been symbolic from its very beginnings, but we can honestly say that it is *inherently* symbolic. It is with this in mind that we should consider the academic attitude towards engineering discussed earlier; in a way it is entirely correct that 'it is more important to signify than to be', because to express engineering purely is to admit to the pre-closure of a certain idea of progress that has been so deeply vital to modern architecture from its very inception.

When engineering architecture returned to the forefront of critical consciousness in the 1920's it would be in a thoroughly aestheticised form. Although political attitudes varied between practitioners, nobody was, nor could be immune to the problems of expression, although all would disavow these problems to a greater or lesser extent. When the iron & glass palaces were being constructed they were in almost direct contradistinction to the aesthetic sensibility of the time.[101] Whereas 1920's modernist architecture would be a branch of similar movements operating within the visual arts. But in the earliest period after the First World War, the problem of 'housing' was the most challenging, and the one given most thought. Architects made themselves famous through building private villas and then publishing them, or by creating manifestoes for the remaking of urban form, theoretical grand solutions to social problems. Making a fetish of the aesthetics of industry would more-or-less fall off the agenda; technocracy would be more of an issue than technology. After the fire of 1936, Le Corbusier would pay tribute to the Crystal Palace and its legacy, mythologizing its utility and lack of precedent, bemoaning the destruction of so many iron & glass buildings, calling the Crystal Palace the 'last witness of that era of faith and daring', praising its 'triumphant harmony', its 'grandeur and simplicity'.[102] In Le Corbusier's tribute, we can see a narrative being constructed that somewhat neglects the iron & glass aesthetics of disappearance, although Le Corbusier admires the scale and the technique, he frames it within his own concerns; it would be 'abstraction' that defined modernism more; instead of fragile skeletons of metal, experiments would be made with floating planes and volumes.

Concurrent with the various strands of modernism developing in their self-consciously avant-garde manner were streams of design thought that far more closely resembled the 'functional' narrative of iron & glass that we saw previously. Partially this was through the construction of mega-structures such as power-stations or factories, and partially through further advances in transport engineering such as the motor car or the ocean liner. Many of the seemingly unpretentious and rational forms of these objects would be held up as models that architects should aspire to in their own work, but this is not to say that there was *no* aesthetic to mega-structures. In fact their bulk, abstraction and seeming unconcern with 'architectural' concerns became a pattern book of symbolically loaded machine-forms that architects could use to signify their modernity.

Where a purer iron & glass aesthetic of some kind would appear at this time would be in the work of the most radical left-wing architects. Takes Hannes Meyer, head of the Bauhaus from 1928-30, who was fired by the mayor of Dessau for donating money to striking workers, and who would design buildings for trade unions as part of a collective practice with his students. His competition entry for the League of Nations (1927, unbuilt) made great play of the egalitarian overtones of modularity and repetitive units; compared to Le Corbusier's heroic modernist entry to the same competition, Meyer's was rough and full of radical commitment, with a gigantic steel and glass dome over the assembly. Kenneth Frampton makes the connection explicit: referring to Meyer's radically democratic deployment of prefabricated units and the privileging of process over composition, he wrote that

> All unity is now seen to reside not in some pre-ordained static ideal, as in antiquity, but in process itself, as made manifest through the proliferation of rationalized technique in response to changing need. Hannes Meyer's design for the League of Nations building of 1927, with its systematic modular assembly of components, clearly intends little else but such a manifestation. In this respect one can hardly overlook its significant derivation as technical method from Paxton's Crystal Palace.[103]

This is a very strong deployment of the aesthetic, naked prefabrication coming to stand as a metaphor for socialist organization.

The other extreme modernist reaction to iron & glass would come from Russia, with the revolutionary architects of the 1920s. As is well known now, in the fervour of the early Soviet period, avant-gardism was encouraged, and various artists and architects unleashed an almost unprecedented level of experiment and creativity. In one sense their visions were assisted by the lack of money and material that civil war ravaged Russia was capable of providing; this scarcity perversely allowed for genuinely fantastical creations to be imagined. In the spirit of Chernyshevsky, constructivists were keen to imbue inert materials with political potential, and the constructivists would frequently designate glass as a material whose transparency was as symbolic as it was physical, the openness of massive frames and structures in tension testifying to the truly democratic and dynamic communism that they were trying to create. This revolutionary symbolism reached its apotheosis in the design for the 'Monument to the Third International' (1919) by Vladimir Tatlin, possibly the most celebrated unbuilt work of architecture of the 20th century. Deeply inspired by the Eiffel Tower, and its associations with the 1789 French Revolution, it would be described by the critic Victor Schklovsky as being 'made of iron, glass and revolution'.[104] A helicoidal steel frame (its spiral form evoking the progressive syntheses of the dialectical method) would soar 400m into the sky above Leningrad, into which a number of gigantic revolving glass units containing the programme would be suspended. Famously the proposal required more steel than the whole of Russia was capable of producing at the time, yet there is no other example of the futurism of ferro-vitreous construction being used with such strong political overtones. The wilful yet impossible ambitiousness of Tatlin's Tower, which was at once 'both rigorous and frail',[105] is depicted as a rusting hulk in digital representations,[106] and is frequently described in terms that should now be familiar:

> The more we learn about the tower [...] the more it seems that it was not a "monument" at all. It was instead a constellation of inspiring fragments, dispersed across the century by an artist who dared the future to build something out of the ruins of his dream.[107]

Tatlin's Tower is a perfect example of what we have described as the 'abstract ruin'; suffused with a melancholy that is shorn of its comforting qualities, an injunctive failure.

Despite these revolutionary exceptions however, which

significantly remained unbuilt, concrete would be the primary material in which modernist architecture would be constructed from until well after the Second World War, and even then the glassy aesthetic of Mies van der Rohe and others was a luxurious, almost neo-classical architecture, reflective rather than transparent. Indeed, lacking any transformative symbolism it was tailor made for corporate clients. It was not be until the cultural turmoil of the late 1960s that the radical aesthetics of disappearance would become prominent within architecture again.

Solutionism

The cult of the engineer-genius that began in the 19th century is as strong as ever. In a similar fashion to the conservative view of the Great Exhibition, there is a popular image of this character; a no-nonsense man capable of overcoming insurmountable technical challenges. He is best exemplified by Isambard Kingdom Brunel; a Victorian engineer of bridges, ships, and railways, subject of the iconic photograph showing him nonchalantly smoking a cigar in front of a gigantic chain (from the anchor of his ship the *Great Eastern*). In 2002, when the BBC conducted a survey and produced a television series to find out who were believed to be 'the 100 Greatest Britons ever', I.K. Brunel came second only to Winston Churchill, just ahead of Princess Diana.[108] Again, it is not particularly difficult to know that jingoism is a strong factor in this cultural trope; nostalgia for the period when the UK was indeed the most technologically advanced society in the world is understandable if deeply reactionary; the presence of the right-wing libertine car-bore Jeremy Clarkson as Brunel's champion puts the attitude we are describing into sharp focus. But this vulgar engineer-genius is merely the popular side of another tendency – the same attitude towards the simplicity of motive and freedom of purpose that the engineer supposedly enjoys is visible even in the most modern of architectural histories, and strong and often explicit expressions of continuity are made between contemporary architects and their Victorian predecessors. This particular conceptual relationship to 'construction', whereby it is understood only as a selection of problems of simple delineation and implicit usefulness, is a powerful and, I will argue, a damaging one. It creates a condition whereby the architect or designer sees their role and relevance primarily as a solver of simple problems. Rather than Giedion's '*constructor*', a term which always to some degree carries a notion of political commitment or at least symbolic attachment, we might call this character a *'solutionist'*.

I.K.Brunel, 1857

The original and perhaps purest example of the solutionist is Richard Buckminster Fuller (1895-1983), the legendary engineer-idiot-savant. Fuller's genius is not in question; an eccentric 'boffin' who carefully maintained his position at the periphery of the architectural world, he invented and popularized of all manner of structures such as the geodesic dome and the tensegrity structure, as well as being a pioneering ecologist and life-long educator. He was a man of singular intellect and drive, yet nonetheless he was in possession of a ridiculously pitiful level of political *nous*. Fuller was a theorist of plenitude, who believed that technological advancement could lift humankind from 'the role of an inherent "failure," as erroneously reasoned by Malthus, [to] that of an inherent success'.[109] A technocrat *par excellence,* Fuller saw both socialism and capitalism as outmoded and inadequate systems, run by incompetent and obsolete politicians, and looked forward to the time that 'the industrial equation will bring about a condition where, within a century the word "worker" will have no current meaning. It will be something you have to look up in an early twentieth-century dictionary'.[110] This depressingly ironic vision of a post-industrial society is just one example of Fuller's naïve optimism, and it is not too difficult to discern the performative aspects of it; his concept of plenty is born from his harsh experiences of the great depression, and despite his rallying against war and the state apparatus, a great amount of his work would be completed for the US military. Nevertheless, Fuller was to prove one of the greatest influences on the new wave of engineer-architect visionaries of the late 20th century.

In Britain after the Second World War, the poverty, the relinquishing of its colonies, and the new geo-political paradigm of the cold war all accelerated the decline in its international status. This further confirmation of its decentred position in the world would be thoroughly traumatic for its self-image, accentuating the already sentimental aspects of British culture. But it was also the time that the political establishment was at its most progressive, creating – in the name of modernity – the welfare state and mass social housing. Architecturally, the vital influence at this time in the UK would be Le Corbusier, who was by the end of World War Two entering what is known as his 'late' phase; rather than machine symbolism, his architecture was becoming more monumental, more crude, and in a certain way more mystical, as if forced by the (cultural) traumas of war into retreating from ideas of 'progress' in favour of a gnomic symbolism. At this same time the urban ideas put forth by Le Corbusier and the CIAM *(Congrès International d'Architecture Moderne)* were coming into fruition as all over the world governments made efforts to address the 'housing problem' in their war-ravaged countries. This general soup of ideas would lead in the UK to what you might call the 'welfare state modernism' of mass-housing schemes.

A particular event that should be mentioned here is the Festival of Britain of 1951. Famously held on the centenary year of the Great Exhibition, this would be of much smaller scale than its inspiration, and was primarily for domestic experience. It was an attempt to lift the spirits of a population still subject to food rationing, while also encouraging them to accept their new place in a scientifically oriented world that they were not at the centre of. Although there were campaigns both to rebuild the Crystal Palace for the festival or to use the empty Sydenham site as the location for new buildings, they were both rejected;[111] after the ravages of the war the state wished to place a far greater cultural focus on the future rather than the recent past. One similarity between the two events is their falling upon the cusp of the dissemination of new forms of technology; the Great Exhibition was for many a significant introduction to industrial culture, while the Festival attempted to introduce the viewer to the new scientific culture of atoms and space exploration. It is also worth noting that the Festival of Britain was as equally focused upon the paternalist notion of the education and improvement of the common person as the Great Exhibition had been, but this was different in significant ways; the Festival was based more on a commitment to the working classes rather than a fear of them:

The Great Exhibition was seen in 1851 as a testament to the

free-market and voluntarism (although Chartists and protectionists disagreed), while the 1951 Festival of Britain has often been portrayed as 'a perfect piece of Socialism'.[112]

The architecture of the festival was of a sort that was torn between a concrete modernism and a more engineered aesthetic of exposed steel, which was at once indebted to the Stockholm Exhibition of 1930 and Le Corbusier's *Pavilion de Temps Nouveaux* from the Paris Exposition of 1937, while also being redolent of the ephemerality of the Crystal Palace. So while the Festival would give London polite modernist buildings such as the Royal Festival Hall, it would also feature buildings of more tensile, almost constructivist aesthetic such as the Basil Spence's Sea & Ships Pavilion, Ralph Tubbs' Dome of Discovery and Powell & Moya's Skylon, all of which would be quickly demolished, thus passing into the same nostalgic, fragmented condition of loss that we have seen before. This aesthetic of girders and cables was a main feature of the Festival; evoking the new 'scientific' and technocratic culture of expertise that the government were both reacting to and trying to promote amongst the people, although the only building that would remain after the festival would be the Royal Festival Hall.

While Reyner Banham would later (1976) say 'it is striking how many of [the current] generation have told me in recent months that it was the Festival that turned them on to modern architecture',[113] a generation of British architects who matured in the fifties would find the Festival twee and inappropriate. Notable amongst these were Alison and Peter Smithson, whose links to pop-art via the Independent Group and notions of place and material were more intellectual and serious than the picturesque Festival Style. The Smithsons became famous for the approach known as 'New Brutalism', which would eventually become one of the most reviled architectural movements of the twentieth century, for what are only *partially* aesthetic reasons.

Brutalism was a far cry from 'solutionism', predicated as it was upon materiality, specificity and place. It was conceived as a form of timeless architecture, speaking of a 'functionalist tradition' that could stretch back to pre-history. Its execution eventually tended towards heavy monumentality and bespoke megastructures, both of which conditions set brutalism far apart from the ferro-vitreous architecture of the previous century.

The first significant 'solutionism' in Britain would be that of Archigram, a loose-knit group of radical architects based in the UK who made their name through the self-publication of a number of magazines from the late 60s into the early 70s. Their work was a mix of swinging-sixties pop-culture, sci-fi fantasy, hyperactive conjecture, and an obsession with 'newness'. Their general tendency was to aim towards the obsolescence of architecture, both in the use of the latest in technology to de-monumentalise building, but also to allow environments to be responsive to the individual consumer; a key concept of theirs was 'indeterminacy'. They promoted projects featuring 'plug-in' cities of plastic dwelling units lifted around by cranes, pneumatic 'homes' that could be carried around on the back of the consumer, and 'walking cities' that could travel around the world to any location. Archigram were just one of a number of European architectural groups that were ploughing similar furrows in this period, but in comparison to groups like Austria's *Co-op Himmelblau,* or Italy's *Superstudio,* and in line with Buckminster Fuller, Archigram were relentlessly positive and politically naïve: if something was new, it was therefore good; it was up to others to be political.

'The experimentalist may come to be some kind of special force in the wake of social change, but not necessarily part of its avant-garde';[114] wrote their most vocal member Peter Cook, stressing the disavowal of engagement that one always finds in the solutionist. Indeed, Archigram were in thrall to the very idea of the engineer-genius: 'What fascinated Archigram's generation were the eccentric, proactive qualities of engineering, the way in which the 19th century exhibition structures [...] were conceived as kits-of-parts, temporary and "live"'.[115] This might sound somewhat akin to the efforts of Hannes Meyer we mentioned previously, but rather than actually engaging with the complexities of their culture, Archigram relied on the radical associations that being 'into' the newest of the new would bestow upon them, in an almost pure example of consumer capitalism. Cook would stress the case for 'solutionism' by eulogising the engineer-genius thus: 'His is the tradition of Invention or, more precisely, of the attitude of mind that solves problems by inventing ways out of them'.[116] But as we have seen, Archigram could not help but be trapped in the world of aesthetics – they only built two small buildings (one of which was a swimming pool for the rockstar Rod Stewart), and so the visionary 'look' of their conjectural work would be their biggest legacy for generations to come; poppy, vibrant, aesthetically rich but conceptually shallow. Their influence can also be felt through their pedagogy: all of Archigram taught, and many famous architects of the next generation would pass through their studios. One can see the Archigram influence in the school that Peter Cook ran at UCL in London from 1990 to 2005; under his command he developed a diverse, graphically virtuosic but – again – naïve culture often marked more by fascination than engagement. In fact, if we wish to follow the stream of Archigram thought to its logical conclusion, we arrive somewhere somewhat less avant-garde. There is literally no better spatial embodiment of Archigram's obsession with transience, fun, media entertainment and spectacle than the pop-up cities of the music festival – fifty thousand middle-class people in a field staring at Bono is where the Archigram version of utopia takes you.

The 'movement' that circulated around Archigram was known as 'Zoom'. On the one hand this could describe the people involved to various degrees in the movement all across the world, but it could also refer to the shared interests of the protagonists; ephemerality, gadgetry, indeterminacy, anti-monumentalism. As previously mentioned, Archigram never made their mark in terms of real buildings; their breakthrough project for an entertainment centre in Monaco was a victim of the oil crisis of the early seventies. Indeed; the kit-of-parts future that was supposedly just around the corner never managed to become economically or politically viable. The closest attempt to create a building that was an embodiment of the 'Zoom' ethos would be completed not by Archigram, but by their contemporaries, Renzo Piano and Richard Rogers. The Pompidou Centre (1971-) in Paris marks a transition between two different sensibilities – it is both the most significant attempt to create a 'Zoom' building, and also the beginning of what is known as the *'British High-Tech'* movement in architecture; a sensibility marked by 'solutionist' attitudes in much the same way as Archigram were, but that unlike 'Zoom' has been implemented on a very large scale, all over the world.

The Pompidou Centre marks the largest attempt to elaborate the theoretical and practical concerns of the period in a single building; and we can compare it to the Crystal Palace in a number of interesting ways: both were commissioned by the state, both were conceived within the context of periods of social unrest, both called for an unprecedented programme of display (the Pompidou Centre was to be an art gallery, but an art gallery stripped of the institutional elitism associated with that particular typology; rather, it was to be the first 'cultural centre'). Finally, both were 'radical' designs by relative outsiders, won through public competition. Rogers and Piano's winning design was filled with 'Zoom' ideas; the concept hinged upon notions of flexibility; the building would be a massive shed with little or no internal division; massive moveable internal spaces serviced entirely from their periphery would be created; the designers would merely provide the space for 'events', with all the post-68 connotations that the word brought up. Although Rogers had no specific connection to Archigram, he was teaching at the Architectural Association at the time that Archigram were most influential there, and was concerned with similar ideas; we can see germs of the Pompidou in Cook's *Plug-In City*, Warren Chalk's *Ocean*, and Archigram fellow-traveller Cedric Price's *Fun Palace*.

The problems of the Pompidou are well known; the much-vaunted flexibility was compromised from the very start, budgets and regulations led to static floors and partitioned halls and the exposed services led to massive maintenance costs. We find here the problem of the 'solutionist' denial of aesthetics: no matter how much the rhetoric might speak of indeterminacy, what actually came about was that 'the Piano and Rogers team managed to erect the *monument* to the zoom wave'.[117] As well as this there were conceptual problems; just as the Great Exhibition can be analysed as marking a fundamental shift, the birth of the modern consumer, the Pompidou Centre can signify the shift into the postmodern world of consumption. Jean Baudrillard would say: 'Beaubourg represents both the fact of culture and the thing which killed culture, the thing it succumbed to, in other words, the confusion of signs, the excess, the profusion'.[118] And true enough, this new paradigm of culture-machine would indeed spread massively towards the end of the century, but of course without the unpredictable freedom that was the original intention; we will investigate further this phenomenon of the 'brand museum' in the next section. But here I think we should go further; the failure of the Pompidou Centre is marked deeply by certain problems previously mentioned.

The spaces created inside the Pompidou were massive, and although they were by no means as large as the Galerie des Machines, this sublime over-provision of space was noted by commentators at the time.[119] Mezzanines had to be built to divide up the seven-metre high spaces, and partitions drifted far beneath the distant ceiling; once again the melancholy sense that we cannot live up to our own abilities. Alongside this we should again stress that the 'solutionist' narrative – although obviously not the *cause* of the failure – leaves the architects vulnerable to any kind of reconfiguration of the cultural message of their work. The problem of 'solutionist' naivety, which the Pompidou Centre is highly representative of, is exemplified by the following quote:

> This attitude assumes that architecture has no further task other than to perfect its own technology. It turns the problem of architecture as a representation of social values into a purely aesthetic one, since it assumes that the purpose of architecture is merely to accommodate any form of activity which may be required and has no positive attitude toward these activities. It creates institutions, while pretending that no institutionalisation of social life is necessary.[120]

As previously noted, the Pompidou Centre can be read as a spatial manifestation of the transition to postmodern culture. And again, like the Crystal Palace, the radical spatial language *hinted* at by the Pompidou Centre would be subjected to an almost instant reactionary movement: by the time that the Pompidou Centre was completed in 1977, Charles Jencks had published his *Language of Post-Modern Architecture,* which identified the end of the modernist dream of the city. Over the next fifteen years, roughly coinciding with the Reagan and Thatcher periods, architecture found itself in another revivalist period. In an aesthetic restoration akin to the 1893 Columbian World's Fair, whose iron-frames were dressed up in neo-Palladian folderol, an architectural paradigm of up-to-the-minute guts concealed under historicized skin was soon to arrive, and ironic reference and all-out pastiche were the order of the day.[121] Although this turn was, as we shall see, not *entirely* reactionary, the vulgarity and ostentatious cheapness of much postmodern architecture was the perfect reflection of the political climate in which it was created.

In the background, British High Tech was still practised throughout the eighties, most notably by Richard Rogers and Norman Foster. In the sixties they had worked together after studying in the USA at Yale, a period of time in which they became overcome with a similar over-optimistic vision of America to that which had enthralled Archigram. This turning-away from the 'problem' of Europe towards the disingenu-ousness of American innocence is typical of 'solutionism'; in the words of Rogers:

> Returning to Britain to set up our first architectural practice [...] we realised the importance of the American experience where the architect is a genuine problem-solver rather than a mere stylist. We understood that the traditional European approach, constrained by cultural and formal conventions, could never meet the needs of a changing society that we were going to try to serve.[122]

On the one hand this is an understandable approach; an attitude towards 'pure' utility not yet pricked by the critiques of postmodernism, a rejection of the groaning weight of history and of rubble piled upon rubble, a ludicrously naïve faith in the benign nature of technology and American culture. Perhaps most significantly, we see here a total abdication of responsibility. One of the most pernicious aspects of the solutionist narrative is the idea that by declaring something to be insignificant, it will indeed vanish; but time and time again in architecture one can see that the cheerfully optimistic dismissal of mere trifles such as 'style' or 'culture' or 'form' leads to an easy re-appropriation. As previously mentioned; architecture cannot help but be signif-icant, and it can be damagingly naïve to deny that the 'meaning(s)' of a building are not the architect's concern.

Lloyd's Building, Richard Rogers, 1986

After designing Lloyd's of London (1986-), which is perhaps the most stylistically avant-garde building built in Britain in the 20th century, yet commissioned by one of the most establishment clients, Rogers would design a small number of buildings and factories in a mannered, guts-out style, all dressed up in tension cables. He would also become involved in politics; getting close to the Labour party and think tanks and publishing manifestoes calling for the reinvigoration of inner cities after generations of suburban flight. Foster on the other hand would be working hard, more obviously toning down the flamboyant aspects of the high-tech aesthetic into something more sensible, more 'tailored'. But apart from a few major commissions, often for corporate clients, the High Tech movement (including others such as Nick Grimshaw, perhaps the contemporary architect whose debt to the 19th century engineer-genius is most readily admitted)[123] was a sideline, keeping the dream of functionalism alive in the face of an architectural culture hooked upon 'pomo'.

But in the 1990s, High Tech triumphed, for a number of reasons. The recession of the early years of that decade hit the construction industry hard, which, along with the rise of neutered social democracy in the form of the 'third way', meant that 'pomo' architecture was effectively killed off; the apparent seriousness of the mutated High-Tech style – as by then dominated by Foster – was far more palatable than an ostentatious and often tacky architecture that was all too reminiscent of the vulgar 'yuppie' culture of the 1980s. This success was heightened by the adaptation of a High Tech language for the construction of various airports around the world as flying became ever more popular as a means of travel (this is worth comparing to the construction of iron & glass railway sheds), as well as the ever increasing economic reliance on service industries and offices rather than industry. The tightly detailed, slick and shiny architecture that High Tech had evolved into would become the architecture of choice for world commerce. In this corporate language, glass signifies a certain kind of luxury, as well as a democratic 'transparency' that attempts to conceal the unaccountable murk of the world of finance.

Perhaps one of the last buildings to be built in the original High-Tech style would be the Millennium Dome (1999-), designed by Rogers. No single building quite embodies the early 'New Labour' years of 'Cool Britannia' in Britain than this one. It was commissioned for yet another exhibition, this time the 'Millennium Experience', which like the Festival of Britain had been a topic of discussion under a Tory government, but would massively increase in scale when the Labour government took power. The Millennium Experience is remarkably similar to both the Great Exhibition and the Festival of Britain, although each has a character reflective of the preoccupations of its time; the internationalist bravura of the Great Exhibition contrasted with the parochialism of the Festival of Britain, which the Millennium Experience contrasted to both in its individualism: in the words of one commentator: 'After "them" (1851), and then "us" (1951), it is now "me"'.[124] The Millennium Experience failed to live up to the expectations of its creators, indeed, before the traumas and betrayals of the post September 11th period, 'the Dome' was the figure of much of the vitriol aimed at the New Labour government, their ludicrous optimism and vacuous PR machinery, after the costs ballooned and the people mostly stayed away. For much of the remaining decade the building sat forlornly at the edge of post-industrial London, its utterly massive internal space mocking any attempts to fill it, but eventually it was finally taken over and has become the O2, an entertainment venue.

Although the building has not been relocated, the parallels with the Sydenham Palace are remarkable; in the centre of the Dome is now a massive concert venue (whose capacity of 23,000 is virtually identical to that of the Handel Orchestra). The Dome also has a smaller concert venue, and an assortment of bars and cafes, much like the Sydenham Palace. In fact, in a remarkable echo of the 'court' system from the palace, the Dome now has entire 'streets' of false buildings lost underneath the roof far above. But there's nothing artistic or 'improving' about these; the internal architecture of the Dome is vulgar Miami-mall-moderne;

one is almost nostalgic for Victorian condescension and hypocrisy in the midst of all the horrendous barked incitements to 'ENJOY' plastered all over the walls, a perfect example of the 21st century ideological imperative. But at the same time there is a strange quality to the Dome, the skin filtering out most of the daylight, creating a constant crepuscular feeling within the building akin to the 'dirty and sad' light that Benjamin saw in the arcades.[125] But there doesn't appear to be a utopian moment worth clutching here; it's almost as if the transition from the Millennium Experience to the O2 missed out upon the most fantastic and visionary aspects of the Sydenham Palace entirely; it is difficult to see how anyone will be writing eulogies to the Dome as the architecture of the just-future.

Millenium Dome, Richard Rogers, 1999

After the Dome project, Rogers would find himself at the centre of built environment policy making. He would compose manifestoes such as *Cities for a Small Planet,* and as part of the 'Urban Task Force' he would create *Towards an Urban Renaissance* (1999), a key document in the regeneration bubble of the early 21st century, arguing for the densification of cities, sustainable public transport and public spaces. At the same time as this, his architecture had softened to become a gentle, polite reflection of his early projects. The once renegade High Tech approach had cooled down to become what we might remember as Blairite-Modern, welcoming and polished, but cheap and lacking in both substance or morals. The style of this neo-functionalist archi-tecture would be defined by a certain terrified refusal to make a decision; housing blocks, by now generally built with concrete frames (quite the opposite of the 'Zoom' ideal of prefabrication), would be draped in multi-coloured curtain walls and cheap timber panelling, with 'luxury flats' built by private developers that would be smaller than the dreaded council-houses of the generation before. The multitudes of spindly atria and oxidized curtain walls of the last generation of office blocks built all over the world are very much the children of Foster and Rogers, as are the endless sterilisations of once interesting spaces in the name of regeneration. The high-tech spaces we walk through now are fit only for the smiling ghosts of computer visualizations, a purgatory of 'aspirational but accessible' restaurants and bars, 'media-walls' and 'public art' of unremitting dreariness. Where socialists and radicals could once read within the language of explicit engineering signs of redemption or change, the post High-Tech architecture in our cities has no such associations: it may not be historicist, like the postmodern architecture of the neo-liberal turn in the 1980s, but rather its anaesthetized formal language is a perfect complement to the hollowed out shell of social democracy.

However; there are moments that the dreams of the

'solutionist' avant-garde have come closer to fruition than any other time, but never in the way they were hoped. One might be reminded of the Lacanian dictum 'do not give me what I ask for, because that's not it'. It is not my intention to *blame* architects for the cultural problems that attend their work, but it is my contention that the 'solutionist' narrative leaves the architect vulnerable; the much vaunted futility of the designer in the face of political and economic forces is no excuse for capitulation; architects should not be afraid of failure.

Ironically, the focus on a language of efficiency is something that has worked both for and against High-Tech, inasmuch as it was never really genuinely *about* efficiency. One of the reasons that the British High-Tech architects failed to get much built initially was because their work was too bespoke – it cost a lot to construct something that looked so efficient. The American 'can-do' attitude that influenced High-Tech so much actually manifested itself in the speedier and cheaper working methods that would come to Britain (in postmodern clothes) with the corporate architects of the Canary Wharf development (such as Skidmore Owen and Merril, or Kohn Pederson Fox), and would eventually morph into the contemporary Design & Build contracts and Private Finance Initiative (PFI). These streamlined and efficient legal structures have accelerated the descent of architects from their previous position as 'professional' persons of – at least some – standing, towards a job that we might call 'exterior designer': dislodged from their privileged relationship with the client, and now subordinate to the contractors themselves. This is not necessarily a negative development; 'the Architect' has only existed since the Renaissance after all, but this contract revolution has led to some of the most worthless buildings we've seen in living memory, in many ways as bad as the results of corruption in state-funded housing of the 1960s and 70s; class-cleansing 'luxury' tower blocks have been rammed into 'vibrant' areas, while new hospitals, schools and prisons are now almost indistinguishable in their cheapness. That this has happened with so little resistance is at least partially due to the abdication of responsibility that goes hand in hand with a 'solutionist' ideology.

The question of what happened to the prefabricated future would be one that would vex many over the next few generations. One of the most brilliant and sustained inquiries would be that of the filmmaker Patrick Keiller. His 'Robinson' films, *London* (1992), *Robinson in Space* (1997) and *Robinson in Ruins* (2010) are investigations into history, geography, literature and spatial culture suffused with a committed melancholy suggestive of Benjamin's urban studies updated for the post-'68 generation. Keiller notably structures his studies around a fictional narrative concerning an unnamed narrator and an invisible character called Robinson, in the process creating a vivid mix of materialist history and romantic memory. A student of architecture during the 'Zoom' period, Keiller is part of a generation who trained in the belief that the dreams of prefabrication, of the lightweight future and all the freedoms and progress that that implied were just around the corner. His films of the early 1990s are thoroughly shot through with political despair, a sense of having been cheated out of a future, first by the economic turmoil of the 70s and then the right-wing reaction of the 80s. Peppered with vitriolic rants against the 'suburban' Conservative government and their neglect of the city, a major feature of the films is the class war and how it is spatially manifested in the opposition between the city and the countryside. The *Robinson* films each pose a single 'problem' – a thematic as well as academic device. *London* focuses around questions of the apparent decline of the capital city, and the question of the seeming impossibility of an artistic and social modernity arising from within it, *Robinson in Space* is an investigation into the spatial artefacts of the supposedly immaterial capitalism of the late 20th century, while *Robinson in Ruins* looks at the role of the countryside in the development and reproduction of English capitalism itself. *The Dilapidated Dwelling* (1999), although not a 'Robinson' film, should be seen as part of the same line of enquiry. In this case, the question posed is 'why does the production of housing never become modernized?' By framing his investigation into 'the home' as such, Keiller attempts to avoid the cul-de-sac of monumentality; for if the *'Zoom'* ethos had a radical core at all, it would be in the form of a revolution in everyday life, driven by new modes of dwelling, as made possible by technology.

The narrator travels around the UK interviewing various figures such as Martin Pawley, an architecture critic with 'Zoom' pedigree, the radical geographer Doreen Massey, and Cedric Price. They watch archive footage of Buckminster Fuller, Archigram and Constant Nieuwenhuys, and try to ascertain why the building trade produces so slowly and in such an outmoded fashion compared to other consumable objects. What is suggested, and what is relevant to us here, is that the reasons why the prefabricated, temporary, flexible and ephemeral future never occurred are ideological ones. When asked why the housing trade is not modernized, Pawley uses the remarkable metaphor of a bank note; an object made of the most banal of materials, yet encrusted in detail; its symbolic value graphically reinforced with ideologically loaded imagery. What is the point of accelerating and modernizing the production of housing when the house is the locus of so many of our desires for permanence, the physical manifestations of our spectral wealth, and the place in which the institution of the family is contained and repro-duces itself? The answer lies not in technology itself, and not in the naïve 'solutionism' of Archigram, who are overheard asking the utterly ludicrous question; 'we can build aeroplanes, cinemas that travel at 500 miles an hour in the sky, why don't offices do the same?' The answer that 'solutionism' cannot grasp is that a technological revolution is nothing without a political one.

And yet in Keiller's films he does find traces of the prefabricated future; but he finds it in unlikely places, for example the massive distribution sheds that store consumer goods as they are moved around the country, the points in which ghostly capitalism actually *becomes solid*. Against the hyper-aestheticised technology of the 'solutionist', these buildings are large and featureless; they are almost invisible, not through transparency but through their distinct lack of aesthetic. Recently, Chris Petit's film 'Content' (2010) attempts to aesthetically approach these almost entirely blank spaces. In the words of Petit, the big sheds 'render architecture redundant'. One is put in mind of Giedion's caption for a photograph of the rudimentary walkways on the roof of the Bon Marche: 'When the nineteenth century feels itself unobserved, it becomes bold'.[126] But is it possible to imagine now reading radical possibilities into these forms whose minimal-aesthetic fails to meet any of the usual criteria of 'architecture'? Can we really eulogise these architectural objects that are monuments to our very lack of industry?

InterAction Centre, Cedric Price, 1976

Time and again we have encountered what appears to be a loop, whereby the profession of functionalist principles oscillates with a simultaneous re-aestheticisation. It would seem that the solutionists of 'Zoom' and then 'High Tech' would all too readily fall into this loop, losing their political bearings in the process; for example, Archigram 'recognised formal power in the very antiforms with which Buckminster Fuller tried to repel architectural form, and stepped in to avert aesthetic disaster'.[127] While the breakthrough project of Foster and Rogers (as Team 4, along with Wendy Cheesman and Su Brumwell), a factory for Reliance Controls (1967-90) 'marked the point at which the structural rationality proclaimed by High Tech architects lapsed into exaggeration and expressionism – i.e. at its very birth'.[128] We have of course already seen how the Victorians were well aware of this problem, from the very beginning of mass-produced architecture. But there is something else; if this aesthetic loop is foreclosed, there are some aesthetics that are more particular than others; for example, we might take a look at the designs of Buckminster Fuller, but their calculated 'antiforms' were found incredibly attractive by the young 60s generation – the geodesic dome was a stylish and memorable icon of technological progress. On the other hand we could consider the aesthetic of Cedric Price (who we have already mentioned with regard to the influence of his unbuilt Fun Palace project on the Pompidou Centre). Cedric Price was in some ways perhaps the ultimate 'solutionist' – he had the required faith in technology and the belief in a changing society, but his was not the flippancy of Archigram; his projects were based on a level of rigour that was a world apart from his fellow 'Zoom' architects. Price was well known for commitment to indeterminacy, his aversion to style, his absolute rejection of monumentality and detail. Bearing in mind that a non-aesthetic is still an aesthetic, if we examine Price's built work we can begin to see remarkable parallels with the iron & glass palaces, with their immateriality and their un-ruined dilapidation. Price's Aviary at London Zoo (1961-) is a spacious wire tent, based upon a Buckminster Fuller tensegrity structure, so immaterial as to be almost non-existent. Filled with trees, it was intended to be quickly removed once the birds had made their permanent home, but is still standing, dirty yet proud. His Fun Palace project is very similar to the system of courts we discussed inside the Sydenham Palace; a minimal superstructure was to be filled with a shifting set of fragmented spaces for various leisure purposes. But while the courts of the Sydenham Palace were nominally static, the Fun Palace was to be structured in such a way that it could be reconfigured at any time. The InterAction Centre (1976-2003) was a scaled down version of the ideas from the Fun Palace. A lightweight and stripped down frame was constructed into which containers and other industrial objects were inserted to create an evolving and adaptable set of activities. Again, the comparisons to iron & glass are telling; the spindle-like frame, the sense of potential for expansion and contraction, the incomplete spaces made up by fragmentary units within, the dirt and grime that collected around the permanently-temporary structure, all these things were visible in the Crystal Palace at Sydenham, while the programmatic concerns of activity and delight were modern versions of the 'People's Palace'. Price built little, and would probably reject this assessment of his work, but I suggest that what you can see there is an example of what a genuine future would look like, if the revolutionary change of the late 60s had been more successful. Dirty but not ruined, dream-like and un-monumental – Fantastically dreary.

Iconism

In the last section I noted the origins and decline of the high-tech style which has become the corporate architecture of choice in this new century. But there is another aspect to the current architectural conjuncture which we should investigate, a phenomenon commonly known as 'the Icon'. Here we will investigate the development of 'the Icon' from its roots, tracing out certain significant aspects of its intellectual and cultural development, before finally examining its apparent metamorphosis into a new digital-functionalism.

The ways in which our previous studies of iron & glass buildings and 'solutionism' are relevant here are manifold. On the one hand, the origins of this architectural phenomenon bear familial resemblance to many of the conceptual ideas that have already been deployed in the course of this study; it is important to consider these, as crucial differences in approach have, I will argue, made a very large difference to outcomes. As well as this, previously remarked upon aspects of the relationship of architecture to display and commodity will be examined; the story of the Crystal Palace will be instrumental in shedding light upon 'the Icon' as a cultural phenomenon. Also, it will be seen that the practices developed in the previous twenty years have led to the arrival of what would wish to be considered a new paradigm of architecture; a new synthesis of formalism and functionalism. The previous studies of this text will be seen to be vital here, both in terms of the concept of engineering and the relationship of theory to architecture.

The course of this development is roughly understandable in three periods of architectural production; the first is the development of what became nicknamed 'decon' (short for 'deconstruction' or even 'deconstructivism'); an exuberant formal architecture that grew in contradistinction to both 'pomo' and

'High-Tech' architectures, and was famously linked, for better or for worse, to various trends in post-structuralist philosophy. The second period is thought to begin with the building of the Bilbao Guggenheim Museum (1997-) by Frank Gehry, marking the sudden transition from 'decon' to what has become known as 'iconic' architecture. At this point the architects that were considered challenging and even 'avant-garde' would become the most famous in the world due to their being increasingly commissioned to build large prestige buildings for cultural institutions. This development continues to the present day, although there have been intimations of its collapse due to the financial crisis of 2008 onwards. And from within this milieu we are now seeing the development of a new methodology of design, as the digital technologies that were introduced and experimented with in the 1990s have been disseminated widely enough to be substantially effecting contemporary practice.

While in the previous section we concentrated on the long-term development of ideas regarding the symbolic language of engineering, how iron & glass architecture was represented, and what figurative and narrative role it played in ideologies of architecture, this section might seem to drift somewhat from the previous investigation; but it is important to trace this movement for a number of reasons. Although there are no obvious historical links to the iron & glass palaces claimed by the practitioners and theorists of 'decon', it will be seen that through the evolution of its ideas it leads us forward to a strange neo-functionalism; an architecture of the digital revolution rather than the industrial revolution. This section will thus begin to provide a background for understanding this development. Furthermore, within the context of this study of a melancholy modernity in architecture, 'decon' is significant because it represents what might be understood as an attempt to create a 'critical' architecture, a criticism that has superficial resemblances to the one being enacted here – in a way, 'decon' attempted to create an architecture that in its own way was already 'failed'. That this attempt itself 'failed' through its own success is a development that is of significance, and we will try here to understand why this might be.

We have already mentioned the paradigm shift of the 1970s, when postmodernism 'arrived' in architecture, manifesting itself as the opening up of the architect's pattern-book of form to include the languages of antiquity once again. The wider context to postmodernism was partially the massive expansion of the mass-media environment, the political and intellectual ferment of the *soixante-huit* generation and the much vaunted 'end of grand narratives' – the sustained critique of teleological thought which can be at least partially understood in the context of left-wing European intellectuals being trapped between a Washington and Moscow that they equally refused. One strange factor is that within architecture, with its very different notion of 'modernism', postmodern critiques often came from more conservative positions rather than from left-radicals; by the early 70s the conservation movement had begun, reacting against wholesale redevelopment of urban areas, and the destruction of the existing communities therein. There was also growing criticism of certain aspects of post-war mass housing; for example, the partial collapse of the system-built Ronan Point tower block in May 1968 in the UK, or the demolition of the Pruitt-Igoe housing blocks in April 1972 in the US are both seen as pivotal moments in the reaction against 'modern archi-tecture'.[129] The complicated issue of why many mass-housing experiments eventually resembled the slums they had replaced was reduced to the utterly simplistic conceit that 'architects imposed their values on a public that did not share them';[130] a drastically wilful distortion of the politics of building (since when have architects commissioned themselves?) that excused the critic from attempting to properly grapple with the cultural, economic, and ideological aspects of the problem. These criti-cisms of 'modernist' architecture and its supposedly elitist, totalising, or even totalitarian aspects are initial symptoms of the general rightward political drift that would be consolidated a decade later: indeed, the arguments are still being made to this day. Criticisms of modernism made by intellectuals such as Charles Jencks would later be echoed by buffoons such as Prince Charles, and it is a testament to the success of this rightward drift that the *aesthetic* of modernist architecture is – in the popular imagination at least – conceptually sutured almost inextricably to criticisms of socialist ideas about how the city should be organised. In fact, the infantilised quasi-modernism discussed in the previous chapter can be seen as architects' pre-emptive self-censorship, an attempt, after the conservative onslaught of previous decades, not to offend anyone at all, ever. But this is not to say that postmodern critiques of modernist architecture were always launched from the right; for example, architect/theorists such as Venturi and Scott-Brown would argue that it was harmful for architects to dogmatically insulate themselves from more populist languages of design such as those which werefound in mid-'60s Las Vegas, an argument that was compatible with a commitment to state-built mass-housing and other still-radical ideas.[131]

However, there was another vein of postmodern critique that was growing in the 1970s, one which was less concerned with reconnecting with vernacular or popular forms, and more with self-consciously constituting a new avant-garde position within architecture. Rather than being centred around a single academic environment, as was the case with Archigram and 'Zoom' archi-tecture,[132] this loose group of architects and writers were collected around the New York based journal *Oppositions*, which gave voice to a large number of architecturally focused intellec-tuals throughout the 1970s, and was the testing ground for many of the theoretical issues that still resonate throughout architec-tural culture today. We should note that one of the key influences on the *Oppositions* scene was the growing popularity of 'theory' in

US academia. 'Theory' is a term referring to (mostly) post-1968 Continental European philosophy, whose network of influences and references, as well as style and tone, was markedly different to the 'analytical' philosophy popular in the English-speaking world at the time. As various texts began to be translated into English, 'Theory' became very popular in academia in the US, at least partly due to its cachet of radicalism; many of the European thinkers studied were emerging from an intellectual culture steeped in Marx and Freud, and were often themselves committed to revolutionary change in society. 'Theory' was disseminated widely in various different fields, although philosophy departments were famously resistant to it: that 'Theory' was viewed by many with great suspicion is testified to by the 'science wars' controversies of the 1990s, when academic scientists mounted virulent attacks on the 'fashionable nonsense' emanating from literary and social theory departments.[133] The seemingly hermetic complexity and difficulty of much 'Theory' writing was seen by some as deeply attractive and by others as deeply suspicious. Despite these controversies, what is certain is that it introduced a new notion of 'radical critique' into architectural culture.

The architect on whom we will be mostly concentrating upon here is Peter Eisenman (1932-). He was one of the editors of *Oppositions*, and of all the architects associated with 'decon', it is to him that the term is most apposite. Although he has built a number of buildings, it is through self-publication and pedagogy that he has had greatest influence over architectural culture; a large number of significant contemporary architects have emerged from his milieu. Contrary to the Boy Scout futurism of Archigram and similar European groups, and also opposed to the historicising tendency of architects like Venturi and Scott-Brown, Charles Moore or Leon Krier, the work of Eisenman has been a life-long attempt to create an autonomous space for architecture, where it can be understood as a self-referential discourse. His intellectual scheme initially owed much to Chomskian linguistics, but he would become well known for the work he created under the influence of Derrida, who is perhaps the most infamous writer of 'Theory'.[134] Making much of the semiotic drift between different contexts for the term 'modernism', in the 1970s Eisenman would call for a 'post-functionalism' for what he described as a 'post-humanist' society. 'Modernism' in his case basically meant abstraction, or a de-centering of man's supposedly central position in the world. Although this de-centering is often ascribed to the 16th century heliocentric discoveries of Copernicus, or the 18th century transcendental philosophy of Kant, Eisenman stated that this de-centering first occurred in the 'modernism' that had developed in various arts at the turn of the 20th century, for example that of Joyce, Schönberg, or Malevich.[135] For some reason Eisenman decided that architecture had an imperative to *also* enact this de-centering that supposedly had not been achieved before. Eisenman would claim with reactionary arrogance that 'function-alism' as a theory of formal expression in architecture was inade-quate, and that 'the primary theoretical justification given to formal arrangements was a *moral* imperative that is no longer operative within contemporary experience'.[136] The upshot of this was that Eisenman believed it his responsibility to work at the interrogation of form-for-form's sake, as a way of subverting what was described as a 'dialectic' of form and function. This puerile nihilism corresponds remarkably well to the juvenile futurism of Archigram – it is tautological in a similar way – for Archigram, technology was good because it was good, for Eisenman 'critique' was good because it was good, never mind what was being criticised and to what ends. It also functions, yet again, as a way of avoiding a wider self-criticism.

What Eisenman was actually achieving during the 1970s was remarkably similar to 'mannerist' architecture of the 16th century – witty games for a clued up audience. His early projects (frequently houses for fellow academics, with a series of portentously abstract titles) threw up such frivolities as upside down staircases and marital beds divided by 'voids' (House VI, 1972-) or even 'inaccessible voids' at the very centre of the house (House 11a, 1978, unbuilt). These formal gambits sometimes developed works of fascinating architecture (such as House X, 1978, or the Guardiola house, 1988, both unbuilt) that resembled a kind of over-elaborate memory of seminal works of modernism by Terragni or Le Corbusier, but Eisenman would never present them in that way, preferring instead to see them as serious investigations into architectural semiotics. In the case of an outstanding mannerist building like the Palazzo del Te (1524-) the architect, Guilio Romano (1499-1546) played games with the classical language that his educated aristocratic client would be familiar with; the slipped triglyphs and broken pediments were created for the purpose of generating intellectual *pleasure* through the breaking of established rules of form, and the simulation of instability; Eisenman's early work utilised remarkably similar means, featuring all kinds of safe, whimsical subversions. The other main strand to his early work was 'artificial excavation': projects that uncovered and recreated layers of history from the site upon which he was working, deploying the metaphor of the palimpsest to create overlapping spatial conditions and aesthetics.

Although often genuinely interesting in and of itself, Eisenman's early work would be dressed up in all kinds of leaden puns; 'The Fin d'Ou T Hous [...] could be read as "Find Out House," "Fine Doubt House," or even "Fin d'Août," the end of August';[137] or in long passages whose style mimicked the opaque and often awkward syntax of Derrida's prose when rendered in English.[138] His cherry-picking of technical language is a method that would be explained by his acolyte Jeffrey Kipnis thus:

Readers well studied in Derrida will no doubt find this practice exasperating, since the words and ideas the architect puts in the philosopher's mouth rarely offer a rigorous representation of the philosopher's actual position and can deviate markedly from it. [...] it is helpful to remember while reading these texts that the accuracy of the architect's reports of Derrida's thought does not in the end matter to the architect's own conjectures. Eisenman does not seek to derive authority or force from his representation of Derrida's position; like any speculation in dialogue form, the reports are but rhetorical devices to help the architect clarify his own position.[139]

The audacity here is impressive; ranging from naivety to disingenuousness. How are we to understand the statement that Eisenman does not seek to derive authority from making appeals to Derrida's name? If no authority is being sought, why would he need Derrida as a foil at all? It would seem that what is going on is that Eisenman is appealing to the proper name 'Derrida', the 'famous philosopher', in order to avoid having to describe his own architectural motivation in simple terms of taste. Derrida here functions as a symbol of protected knowledge – in a gesture that reeks of the worst kind of elitism, his name functions *purely* to add *gravitas* to Eisenman's work. Eisenman is not alone in this behaviour though; since him it has become a pernicious practice in architectural culture (it can be argued that it occurs in this very book!), although it will be seen that other architects have utilised other discipline-slippery means of extracting surplus cultural capital.

This borrowing of philosophical language for no particular reason is, at the end of the day, an example of the cliché of the architect as 'renaissance man' – a worn-out tradition of the architect being supposedly capable of drawing inspiration from any and all fields. That Eisenman operated in a sort of intellectual limbo, on the one hand too esoteric for the majority of architects, on the other not actually making a contribution to cultural theory, is exemplified by the collaboration that was organised between Eisenman and Derrida to create a garden for the Parc la Villete in Paris (1985, unbuilt). The utterly cringe-worthy nature of this failed collaboration is documented in a book; *Chora L Works*; each copy of which *actually has holes cut through it*, presumably as a challenging, avant-garde way of expressing Eisenman's own preoccupation with voids and negative spaces.[140] Throughout the collaboration, documented in a series of letters, drawings, and transcribed conversations, Eisenman is frequently left exasperated by Derrida's repeated return to 'the demands of the real'[141] that runs contrary to Eisenman's quest for abstraction; essentially an architecture without humans, or at least without annoying users.

In fact, in view of what we are about to see in relation to the development of 'decon' architecture, in this early encounter, Derrida himself saw pretty well the problems of bringing theory into architecture as a purely aesthetic device: 'They were just using words and the code which is not architectural, and they are just using philosophical, theoretical tools borrowed from deconstructive texts and trying to say something which is not, strictly speaking, deconstructive', as he would admit soon afterwards.[142] Indeed, by the end of their collaboration it was quite clear that Derrida had had quite enough, sending a remarkable recorded message (note the spectral subjectivity) and text to be played out at a conference, ostensibly as a stimulus for discussion. Derrida's recording/letter, hinges around a series of questions that he poses to Eisenman, questions that attempt to put into the realm of doubt many of the claims that Eisenman makes in his texts about architecture; but questions that are especially significant for us in its relevance to our previous study of iron & glass.

As might be expected, Derrida takes issue with Eisenman's desire to 'remove architecture from the measurement of man', his safe flirtation with tropes of disintegration and destruction, and specifically asks him to consider this in the context of genuine connections between 'architecture and capital', 'architecture and war', 'housing' and 'homelessness'; essentially, the actual social conditions that Eisenman's borrowed language of negativity describes. Derrida next asks Eisenman to consider a text by Benjamin, 'Experience and Poverty'. At first, Derrida notes that there already exists in this text a principle of 'post-humanism', but that it is the post-humanism of the revolutionary, exemplified by the Soviet citizens who named their children 'October': 'for humanlikeness – a principle of humanism – is something they reject. Even in their proper names.'[143] These are admittedly rather crude provocations, but they do show the political void in Eisenman's thought, they highlight the vulgarity of using radical language as window dressing.

Furthermore, Derrida introduces Benjamin's discussion of glass in order to highlight contradictions in Eisenman's notion of traces. The 'trace' in Eisenman is the minimal remnant of a compositional operation on a form, similar to but distinct from the 'imprint'.[144] For Benjamin, the trace is a sign of the Bourgeoisie and their attempts to control history in the face of mass production; whereas a revolutionary attitude (best expressed by Brecht's 'Erase the traces!') sought to sweep historicism away; revealing one of the utopian aspects of iron & glass: 'Objects made of glass have no "aura." Glass is, in general, the enemy of secrets. It is also the enemy of possession [...] They have created rooms in which it is hard to leave traces'.[145] This is admittedly a complicated aspect of Benjamin's work, often in dialectical contradiction with his obsession with the revolutionary power latent in fragments and ephemera, but again, Derrida's intention is to put Eisenman's radicality into question.

Finally Derrida approaches Eisenman's work from another angle; but again utilising Benjamin; the question this time utilises his figure of the ruin.

is there a relationship between your writing on the palimpsest, your architectural experience of memory [...] and "something" like the ruin which is no longer one thing? [And] is your calculation, reckoning of memory not Baroque in this Benjaminian sense, despite certain appearances? Second, if all architecture is finished, if it carries within itself, each time in an original style, the traces of its future destruction, the future anterior of its ruin, if architecture is haunted, that is to say, marked by the spectral silhouette of this ruin, at work even in its base of stone, in its metal or glass, what brings the architecture of these times [...] back to the ruin, to the experience of "its own" ruin?[146]

Let us examine this further. We wrote earlier about the iron & glass palaces being understood in terms of 'abstract-ruins' in which were manifested qualities of fragility, fragmentation and history, all the while lacking the specific associations of the conventional ruin. In one way Eisenman's work was creating another type of abstraction of the ruin, which Derrida picks up on, but without any of the power that Benjamin ascribes to the fragmentary ruin, a power Benjamin describes as 'allegorical'; a revolutionary melancholy or 'a certain mourning in affirmation', as Derrida puts it.[147] The 'abstract ruin' that we have been talking about was inherently anti-monumental; in its intangibility it was anti-archival – it represented an architecture ill-suited to memorialising, and yet in its spectral, ghostly qualities it revealed the truth of monumentality, which is that 'the structure of the archive is spectral'[148] – in other words, the iron & glass abstracted-ruin represents a condition that monumentality seeks to repress. On the other hand, Eisenman's work of architectural memory is figural, it monumentalises forgetting; its fragments *symbolise* forgetting, it *reifies* memory. Derrida's deconstruction of Eisenman's metaphorical language draws to the surface the fact that Eisenman engages in the very memorialising practices that he claims to be subverting. It is worth recognising that Eisenman's later (and most publicly prominent) work, 'The Memorial to the Murdered Jews of Europe' (2004-) in Berlin, would be notable for its almost total abstraction, and strong monumentality.

In a belated response to this letter, Eisenman set out his position in a way which rather proves our point for us; while he chooses not to rise to the bait of Derrida's pompous humility, he does feel it necessary to respond thus:

> How does one assert that certain urgent problems such as homelessness or poverty are no more questions of architecture than they are of poetry or philosophy without sounding callous? These are indeed human problems, but architecture, poetry, and philosophy are not the domains in which they will be solved.[149]

So, at the far end of the conceptual spectrum from the 'solutionist' that we saw earlier, we have another paradigm of denial. Eisenman here exemplifies a position where architectural culture is hermetic, sealed off against the very world that it inhabits. Where the 'solutionist' combines naivety with at least a *concern* for questions regarding the political aspects of architecture, Eisenman's attitude is one of amoral knowingness, irony masquerading as sophistication. Both attitudes create small bubbles in which the architectural practitioner can as smoothly as possible continue their 'critical' career without jeopardising their ability to keep working; both create a comfortable notion of being 'critical' while simultaneously putting much of the cultural dynamics of their work beyond the realm of critique. But we have noted in both these cases that the practitioners were making their careers in ways other than building; in that sense there was nothing to stop them from creating genuinely critical and polemical work; they were protected from the ruthless economics and power structures of the building trade. Instead, both Archigram and Eisenman showed themselves to be conservatives masquerading in 'radical' clothes.

The first major milestone on the way to the creation of an 'iconic canon' came in 1988 with the 'Deconstructivist Architecture' exhibition at the Museum of Modern Art. An ugly portmanteau of 'deconstruction' the intellectual movement and 'constructivism' the avant-garde cultural movement, this show was again curated by the erstwhile fascist Philip Johnson, who in a masterstroke of philistinism managed to de-claw a movement in architecture for the second time in a century (we have already discussed his pivotal role in de-politicising European modernist architecture in the 1930s). However, in this case the architects who were aesthetically neutered were not the architects whose work was being shown (Frank Gehry, Daniel Libeskind, Rem Koolhaas, Peter Eisenman, Zaha Hadid, Coop Himmelblau, Bernard Tschumi), but the revolutionary Russian artists to whom the young designers were being compared. Rather than hailing these young architects as the 'new mannerists' that their work so often resembled, the curators, Johnson and Mark Wigley, tied themselves into rhetorical knots describing the new movement while simultaneously stressing that it was in no way a movement, as well as providing a spectacularly inaccurate history of constructivism. Johnson would lazily admit to being 'fascinated' by the 'diagonal overlapping of rectangular or trapezoidal bars' which apparently to him were a sufficiently all-encompassing link between the two periods,[150] while Wigley would assert that the truly radical period of constructivism was not the post-revolutionary phase of experiments in new typologies for new social organisations, but rather in the early, pre-revolutionary period when constructivism had apparently not yet been 'corrupted by the purity of the modern movement'.[151] In fact, Wigley went even further by stating that through the creation of skewed geometry, 'the traditional condition of the architectural object is radically disturbed'.[152] This shamelessly disingenuous presentation of a politically committed artistic movement would perhaps be amusing if it was not so prevalent; again what we see here is the ironic distance that has become the norm almost all throughout the cultural world. Against the tongue-in-cheek populism of 'pomo', with its gaiety and colourful whimsy, 'decon' presented itself in language such as 'dangerous', 'infected', 'monstrous', 'violates', 'torture', 'frightening', 'shocking', even as a 'nightmare', all the while making very sure that there was nothing remotely threatening about it.[153] As Catherine Cooke noted of the exhibition at the time:

> This insistence that the architecture has nothing to do with other cultural or intellectual shifts of our age runs through to the point of denying fact. [...] Are we to suppose that the Russians also 'challenged the values of harmony' entirely for reasons that 'did not derive from or result in any shifts of culture'? Are we being told that theirs too was merely a hermetic intra-professional game to amuse themselves?[154]

The 'Deconstructivist' show would make those featured famous within the profession, but it would be a decade before they became celebrities outside of the architectural world. During this time they remained mostly as 'paper architects', unable to secure the massive competition win that would secure their careers. This was partly because they had not yet proved themselves as capable; their designs were often of an unprecedented complexity of form, but this complexity also made their designs particularly expensive. In the meantime, some would be most known as theorists (Eisenman and Koolhaas in particular), or teachers and artists (Libeskind and Hadid). It was indeed a difficult time of struggle for the 'decon' architects, but this strad-dling of different media or cultural roles would end up being

very productive for them. As we noted about Eisenman's intellec-
tualism, a character like Hadid could – through the production
of frightfully banal paintings – make an oblique name for herself
by appearing as a painter to architects and as an architect to
painters.[155] Another way that this chameleonic cultural shifting
would be worthwhile for the careers of the 'decon' architects is in
the way that it brought them into the 'cultural milieu'; their
reputations as intellectuals and artists and the faint whiff of
avant-gardism would make them attractive to galleries, to
museums, theatres and other cultural institutions, connections
that they would reap the benefits of in the ensuing decades of
faux-plenty.

Guggenheim Museum Bilbao, Frank Gehry, 1997

Although it is still too early to judge how deep are the long term
effects, the spatial culture of the 'iconic building', which began
with the construction of Frank Gehry's Guggenheim Museum
Bilbao (1997-) has marked another remarkable shift in cultures of
display, potentially as remarkable as that effected by the Great
Exhibition. Of course, buildings have always been iconic – as has
been stressed; a building is always aesthetic, it always has an
ideological register. The most obvious historical precedent for
the 'iconic' building has been the religious building: the

cathedral, grand mosque, etc. has always functioned as a symbol of both ineffable and worldly power. What is new about these temples to culture is that 'the Icon' has turned the museum inside out; it has reversed the hierarchy of the vessel and the objects of display, it has made self-reflexive monuments and exhibitions of emptiness. While the Great Exhibition and the Sydenham Palace both brought the world inside them, displaying industrial and cultural artefacts within their almost dematerialised shells, the iconic museum turns the museum into its content, becoming a display of itself; with 'the Icon', architecture has never been so much of an object. The story of the Guggenheim Bilbao has become a familiar one, repeated again and again around the world. The pattern runs something like this; a city that is suffering from industrial decline, high unemployment, high crime and a diminishing population is rescued by the construction of a signature building which puts the city 'on the map', encouraging investment and stimulating growth (the 'Bilbao Effect', as it is known). Although there is a paradigm for this in the tradition of the international exhibition, or indeed the Olympics (take Barcelona's much vaunted renaissance after the 1992 Olympics), these were examples of massive infrastructural investment undertaken around a significant event; instead, in parallel with the rise of post-Thatcherite social-democracy, with its cynical echoes of the language of previous struggles masking an ideology just as vicious as what came before, the iconic building is supposed to encourage private investment to carry the momentum of regeneration through its sheer magical effects. In the words of critic Jonathan Meades, whose film *On the Brandwagon* is a brilliant indictment of the phenomenon:

There can be no doubt about what type of building will come to be regarded as almost parodically representative of this age. A new type of structure, characterised by its hollow vacuity, by its sculptural sensationalism, by its happy quasi-modernism, and by its lack of actual utility. Yet it possesses two definite purposes, to be instantly and arrestingly memorable, to be extraordinarily camera friendly. This type of structure is a sound-bite's visual analogue. A sight-bite.[156]

With the success of the Guggenheim Bilbao (a success largely measured in the number of photographs taken), we saw the progressive dissemination of what had been previously known as 'decon' architecture, now in the guise of the iconic building. Gone were the pretentions towards danger and radicalism; on the one hand they didn't suit the tone of inclusivity that was now so prevalent, but at the same time the architects didn't need to have that kind of cachet any more; what was needed was nothing more than the old-fashioned artistic-genius persona, by now so vacant as to be laughable. The 'disturbing' forms of decon-struction, without actually changing, now became fun, memorable and accessible to all. From around the world the commissions started to come flooding in, the names of the archi-tects started to trip off the tongues of laypersons (especially as the walls of the icon would invariably be plastered with instruc-tions on just exactly what the architect wanted you to think), every city wanted a piece of the 'Bilbao Effect'. Although in Bilbao, the museum was actually accompanied by the construction of new subway lines and infrastructure (by Foster, no less), in the repetition of the trick there was no need for that; instead we had the mass construction of housing as the property boom reached fever pitch.[157] By the late 2000s, the story had further mutated to something along the following lines – A grasping local government would announce a competition for a cultural building to stand on a piece of derelict post-industrial land, often at the side of a river. Bypassing an excellent if dull scheme by a local firm, the jury would select a world famous architect's generically bespoke design that made some half-baked and utterly spurious reference to the history of the site; the rest of the land in the area would be sold on to property developers to be turned into luxury flats. Variations on this theme would come from the 'emerging' economies: the gulf states have been exceptionally keen to get in on the act of the iconic building, on a scale that would be endearingly crass if it weren't for the autocratic regimes that commission them and the slave labour that builds them. Abu Dhabi has commissioned a number of massive cultural buildings, including branches of the Guggenheim and the Louvre; Dubai's vaulting ambition o'er leaped itself with some of the most ludicrous civil engineering projects and buildings yet seen; and China has been lavishing money on iconic buildings by western architects such as Rem Koolhaas' OMA. Although the economic crash has threatened to cancel out the impetus for the creation of new iconic landmark buildings, especially considering the growing realisation that the wonderful economic benefits of the icon were somewhat chimerical, at the time of writing there are still contracts being signed for the construction of blandly exuberant buildings whose concatenations of fashionable shapes are supposedly intended to evoke 'the natural topography of the Nile valley',[158] 'the organic shapes of a starfish',[159] 'the patterns and textures of ancient Egyptian stonework',[160] 'the petals of a flower',[161] and other such vacuities.

That the Victorian notion of improvement was naïve and patronising is patently obvious. But is there really much of a qualitative difference in the flimsy postures of today's 'starchitects'? The pretentious posing of the 'decon' period has led to a period of entirely juvenile architectural expression; but it is not necessarily their fault. The culture in which they operate has made it thus, the culture of nu-language, the concurrent development of toothless initiates' jargon in both the art-world and the world of government has led to a public realm of unbelievable cretinism. We can scoff at the Victorians and their rational recreation, but who will find utopian sparks in the palaces of banality we have been building? We may find the mid 20th century public art of Alexander Calder, Barbara Hepworth, et al. to be somewhat passé, but is the pathetic capitalist symbolism of public sculpture and architecture, where every new piece of art, every new building feels the need to have not only a snappy nickname but also a plaque to spell out its juvenile symbolism, when public art has been reduced to the level of a fireworks display, an 'ooh-aah' stimulation of the senses lacking any concept whatsoever, is that any better? Again, with post-war modernism there was a genuinely progressive attitude at work; abstract modern art was frequently placed in the centre of housing estates. It may have been paternalist, but there was not the horrid condescension of a culture desperately afraid of being 'elitist'. As happens so often, the repetition of an idea has rinsed it of any content that it may have had in the very first place. Thus many cities have seen the erection of tasteless 'yuppiedromes' in the wake of some 'iconic' catalyst, tower blocks easily as badly designed and built as anything from the post-war period, except constructed by the private sector in the context of 'luxury apartments', with the intention of bringing the wealthy back into the city.[162] *On the Brandwagon* soberingly concludes with footage of the 2005 *banlieue* riots in Paris, suggesting that this repopulation of inner cities with the middle classes is a social disaster waiting to happen. Even if this process of catastrophic degeneration is avoided, the culture that this urban change is an expression of, the political culture of 'spin', of the 'knowledge economy', the artistic culture that supposedly acts as a 'pathfinder' for urban renewal, the architectural culture of the 'icon', of the 'wow-factor', all of these movements are interlinked – they are expressed through monuments that are nothing more than three dimensional logos for empty brands. The development of these regimes of display, from the commodity culture of late 19th century capitalism expressed by the iron & glass palaces and their fragmentation (or making allegorical) of the relationship of subject to object, to the postmodern displays of the Pompidou Centre, 'a supermarket of culture';[163] these all marked the transition towards the 21st century cultural building, the 'museum of nothing'.[164] From the 19th century revelation of glassy transparency it would seem that we have ended up with surface reflection and nothing else.

Virtualism

'High-Tech' and 'Decon' architecture represented two different legacies of the iron & glass palaces; one, the technological narrative that manifested itself in the figure of the engineer-genius, which then gave its structure to the ideology of functionalism and the figure of the 'solutionist', and two, the cultural narrative that led to the super museum, the utterly bespoke and sculptural statement; the inverse of the glass palace, the essence of monumentality. The final section of this study will be to investigate what appears to be a synthesis of these two conditions; catalysed by the dissemination of digital practices in architecture.

The fact that we have not yet mentioned computers is perhaps surprising. We discussed previously the fact that the two Crystal Palaces both played a significant backing role in the history of the development of photography, phonography and television, all of which are *'tele-'* media – projections of subjectivity at a distance, all of which have a 'spectralising' effect. We must understand that the total diffusion of digital media and processes into daily life is another 'spectral' process; one that seems to subsume all the others within itself; we are ever more connected but also ever more distant. The effect of the computer upon architectural culture is contradictory; on the one hand, architecture itself is one of the least spectral of our cultural activities (even as our study is making that very assertion problematic). Architecture, as a kind of archive, acts as a material expression of immaterial information; names, ideologies, cultures; one of its main powers is its potential for stasis and longevity. On the other hand, the Crystal Palace introduced unprecedented ephemerality and fragility into spatial culture, and the 'Zoom' wave sought the absolute dissolution of the monumentality of architecture. We might wonder if the digital revolution would make as spectacular a difference to our experience of space as the industrial revolution did.

In a certain way this *is* what has come to pass; from the early days of the digital revolution we learned of the term 'cyberspace', as coined by William Gibson in *Neuromancer* (1984). The networks of information technology, while manifested within space as the material weight of individual computers or servers, are frequently described as occupying a metaphorical spatial dimension; one that we interact with, but can never actually immerse ourselves in. Despite, or perhaps because of this barred access to the digital, the fictional inhabitation of the metaphorical space of the digital world has been a popular subject for fiction; take the films *Tron* (1982) or *The Matrix* (1999), in which old-fashioned 'brain in a vat' thought experiments are manifested as narratives that question common-sense notions of reality through using the metaphor of total immersion in a digital environment. And now, computer games allow us to inhabit ever-more complex simulations of cities with a physical and moral freedom impossible in the 'meat world'. Nevertheless, compared to the industrial revolution, which genuinely created new forms of space that were unprecedented; department stores, train stations, etc. the digital revolution has not changed space in a tangible way; nearly all of the changes to life patterns that have resulted thus far are still experienced within immediate reach of the body – from the desktop computer to the mobile phone, this revolution in connectivity has made little impact on the discernable fabric of our cities.

The influence of the computer upon the methodology of architecture was slow at first. In a parallel of what Benjamin noted about the introduction of iron construction at first mimicking the forms of wood & stone, [165] the initial introduction of the computer to architecture was as merely the replacement of the pencil and the pen. And even today this is still how the computer is generally used in an architects' office; instead of sitting behind a drawing table with a set-square and an angle-poise lamp, the contemporary architect more often than not spends their time at a computer, using the mouse to create in two dimensions drawings that will be printed out and used by the builder to guide their construction. This may be more efficient than drawing, and it does mean that the sheer amount of work that can be produced is much greater than it was thirty years ago, but it does not mark a qualitative shift in the way that buildings are designed. In order to find a genuine methodological shift in the way architecture is produced, to compare with the changes caused by the development of iron construction, we will have to return to the 'decon' architects of the 1990s.

The original 'decon' exhibition of 1988 featured architecture that was all hand-made; models, drawings, texts, and even paintings. But it would not be long afterwards that the computer made itself significantly felt in the work of these architects; in fact, the early experimental period of digital architecture was dominated by 'decon' architects.[166] This early period should be understood in the context of two main approaches, pioneered on the one hand by Gehry and on the other by Eisenman. Gehry's approach, which we might describe as the 'intuitional' paradigm, is exemplified by his 'Fish' sculpture for the Barcelona Olympics (1992-). This digital paradigm is that of *enabling*- Gehry physically created a form that he wished to create on a large scale, and using software borrowed from the aerospace industry his office were able to design a structural solution that could realise the object. This approach would become Gehry's standard one; indeed, the Guggenheim Bilbao was a massive step up in scale for the use of this method, and was perhaps the most complicated architectural structure yet attempted at the time. This is important to note; in Gehry's method, the architect already knows exactly what they want to create, they have designed something that may be complex, but is entirely within their control; the computer allows them to resolve all of this irregularity *downward* into a construction. In contrast, Eisenman's work with computers by the early 90s, which we can describe as the 'theoretical' approach, was, as you might imagine, far more experimental and self-consciously avant-garde.

By the mid 90s the intellectual fashion in American academia for 'deconstruction' was fading; Derrida was no longer the 'hot footnote', as it were. In his place there was a taste emerging for the radical immanence of Gilles Deleuze and Félix Guattari; the theorists of flows, fluxes and animistic desire. This made its way into the writings of architects as well; most notably in Eisenman but also in the work of a number of other architect/theorists, most of whom had some experience of his New York milieu. As we have seen, Derrida did have an attitude towards information technology; he saw it as a prosthesis, but an extension of the subject that reciprocally robs the subject of their own presence; a making-ghost. Understood in this way the digital revolution does not represent a qualitative shift; it is merely the latest in a series of ostracising effects that can be found in writing, in telephony, in photography, or in the commodity form.[167] On the other hand, the work of Deleuze & Guattari, with its theories of rhizomatic (non-hierarchical, dynamic, even anarchic) networks opposed to arborescent (hierarchical, structured, static, familial) networks, would conceptually map onto electronic systems and digital culture with a vibrancy that would make Derridean theory seem archaic and ill-equipped to explain the cultural paradigm shifts the computer was supposedly bringing about. The frenetic Deleuzo-Gauttarian paeans to flows, to becomings, to schizophrenic processes reflected an impression of digital space as a radically democratic zone of infinite connectivity.

One of the things that made Deleuze & Guattari so popular was their particular way of using language; the sheer number of new (or reconfigured) terms that are coined within *Capitalism and Schizophrenia*, their *magnum opus*, is bewildering; bodies-without-organs, the rhizome, schizoanalysis, the plane of immanence, lines of flight, desiring machines, nomadology, the smooth and the striated, etc. We can understand this partly by looking at their radical background; emerging from the intellectual tumult of 1968, their work is an attempt to pass through what they saw as the negative limitations of theory under the overwhelming influence of Marx and Freud, moving towards the development of a new understanding of capitalism and desire. To achieve this, new terms and new concepts had to be created to break with previous dialectical patterns of analysis. Creativity was privileged over critique. The other side to this ground-up construction of a system was that it was intended to be genuinely inspiring to the reader; Deleuze famously said 'a theory is exactly like a box of tools'; the frenetic and often vague nature of the content of *Capitalism and Schizophrenia* was a call to action rather than further analysis; the breadth of content and subject matter, from mathematics to anthropology to music, made it an incredibly fertile bed in which new ideas were to be planted.

Of all the terms found in Deleuze & Guattari, there were perhaps three that were most influential in architecture; *the fold, the diagram*, and *the virtual*; these would be inextricably linked to the development of digital architecture, and all three of them found prominent voice in the work of Eisenman in the 1990s. The fold as it appears in Deleuze is a term for the behaviour of Deleuze's notion of *multiplicity*, as explained through a study of philosopher Leibniz's theory of monads.[168] Effectively the book is a further exposition of Deleuze's theories of flux, and his resistance to conceptual unity and dialectical thinking. Put more simply; the fold is a metaphor for the way relations within the world are; enfolding is to become more individuated, unfolding is to become more indistinct, all the while resisting the fixed concepts of unity and totality. What is important is that everything is interlinked and changing, even when it is briefly counted as a stable entity. The fold, as it translated to architecture, was partially interpreted as a description of the generation of form, in the words of Eisenman:

> In the idea of the fold, form is seen not only as continuous but also as articulating a possible new relationship between vertical and horizontal, or between figure and ground, thereby breaking up the existing Cartesian order of space.[169]

And partially as a metaphor for the new space-time of the digital realm:

> As we near the end of one era and are about to enter a new one, the idea of the fold presents an opportunity to reassess the entire idea of a static urbanism that deals with objects rather than events. In a media age, static objects are no longer as meaningful as time events; now the temporal dimension of the present becomes an important aspect of the past and the future.[170]

Note here, the discussion of a 'new era'; it is taken for granted here that a technological change necessarily demands a cultural change; perhaps Eisenman is not as far beyond his 'humanist functionalism' as he thinks. In practice, however, this apparent 'breaking-up' of Cartesian space merely led to the complication of the geometry of the projects; Eisenman's work, which in the 1980s had been tied to a system of overlaid plans, thus existing mostly two-dimensionally, now managed to become increasingly complicated and twisted, but still static, monumental.

'The diagram' and 'the virtual' were perhaps more obvious in the way in which they were introduced to architecture, and both would be used in close conjunction. The appeal of the 'diagram' should be self-explanatory; the process of designing a building has nearly always proceeded by way of drawn diagrams from simplest concept to the finest detail. On the theoretical level, the Deleuzo-Guattarian concept of the 'diagram' is based on their concept of the 'abstract machine'; understood in the context of their over-riding refusal of unity in favour of flux, the abstract machine is the definition of a process of pure change;

> an abstract machine is neither an infrastructure that is determining in the last instance nor a transcendental Idea that is determining in the supreme instance. Rather, it plays a piloting role. The diagrammatic or abstract machine does not function to represent, even something real, but rather constructs a real that is yet to come, a new type of reality.[171]

Even this short passage is enough to show that the notion of the Deleuzo-Guattarian diagram is associated with the radically new, and that this ought to be understood in the context of the political dimensions of their work. This notion of the diagram is opposed to what is understood as the traditional diagram; the linear, unidirectional process from simple to complex is anathema to their thought.

In common sense usage the word 'virtual' has come to mean the condition of an object that is represented or simulated on the computer; it can be understood as the *simulacrum* of an object; a cognitive trick played by a computer on the weakness of our senses. A great many of us are familiar with the term 'virtual reality', the concept of an entirely immersive simulated environment. But the *virtual* as understood by Deleuze was in use far earlier, and has a more specific, and complicated meaning; rather than describing the condition of an object represented digitally, the Deleuzian virtual is a part of every object that exists as the structure of the Idea.[172]

> The virtual is fully real in so far as it is virtual. Exactly what Proust said of states of resonance must be said of the virtual: "Real without being actual, ideal without being abstract"; and symbolic without being fictional.[173]

Put more simply; the virtual is a *real* part of any entity that corresponds to its potential for flux, for change. Again, we must understand this in the context of the radically new; the event that shakes reality.[174]

The manifestation of the Deleuzian 'abstract machine' in digital architecture would develop out of the investigations of Eisenman and others in the late 1990s. Around this time, and in a self-consciously experimental manner, software developed for purposes outside of architecture would be brought into the studio in order to create form; most importantly, animation software from the computer game and film industries would by utilised. Experiments would be created where imaginary forces could be applied to a model in the computer that, when animated, would deform its spaces; thus beginning to remove the traditional hand of the 'author' or 'artist' from the resulting design. At first this was experimental in the extreme; Eisenman, for example, would utilise software that mimicked brain wave patterns to design a library (Bibliothèque de L'IHUEI, 1996, unbuilt), or that simulated fluid dynamics to design a ferry terminal (Staten Island Ferry Terminal, 1997, unbuilt). This process makes sense in the way that it utilises the new digital technology to try to create a 'new', indeterminate form of space. However, the limitation is that the 'new space' remains in the computer; the product is merely a strangely shaped building; form for form's sake.

Although deeply experimental, we can actually see here shades of the naïve symbolism of 'the Icon', even in the work of someone as wilfully obscure as Eisenman – the results of the experiments; while somewhat capricious and abstract, are conceptualised through a 'thematic' process – the building's purpose less-than-abstractly dictated the 'abstract machine' to be used. By the middle of the 00s however, this experimental paradigm had greatly matured; on the one hand the arbitrary nature of the early experiments would begin to disappear in favour of a more rational set of digital tools more suited to design; using specific software.[175] The architect could define parameters (size of object, type of geometry, relation to other objects, material strength, environmental conditions, etc.) which would then influence a generated form; making complex and repetitive tasks far quicker (to the extent of making the previously impossible possible), and removing the need for the designer (or engineer, for that matter) to calculate exactly what is going on everywhere in their own design. Most significantly; the designer can change these parameters at any time to completely reconfigure the end results, without needing to repeat any steps themselves; this reciprocity of process is known in various guises as 'scripting', 'genetic algorithms', 'emergent design' or 'parametrics'. It should be noted that this is a massive step forward in terms of the possibilities inherent in the tools of design, but on the other hand, by now these methods were taking the notion of the subordination of the designer to the digital processes to the extreme, effectively bringing about the transformation of the designer from the controller of form to the curator of form, prompting worries about whether 'the role of design has now been transformed into (some would say degraded down to) the equivalent of a prize-dog or a race-horse breeder'.[176] The indeterminacy of these methods can and has been understood in terms of the 'abstract diagram' or the 'virtual'; the fact that the designer has (theoretically) no preconceived notions of form is akin to the 'piloting role' Deleuze & Guattari ascribe to the diagrammatic abstract machine in the process of constructing new realities.

But are these just metaphors? Can we say that the use of attractive Deleuzo-Guattarian rhetoric is actually assisting in the formation of new kinds of space? We should note that this is the condition Deleuze & Guattari would put on any evaluation of the dissemination of their terminology – does it break with existing social assemblages? *Does it constitute a 'line of flight'?* At this point, we should widen our focus again, and admit that, unfortunately, the history of Deleuze & Guattari's influence upon culture has been a rather sad one. If their project was to try to preserve the energy of 1968 into the creation of a new politics, or new forms of subjectivity, then it seems, at this stage anyway, to have failed. The anti-capitalist movement of the 1990s was perhaps the closest the world came to a rhizomatic revolution; street battles setting deterritorialised groupings of nomadic activists in Seattle and Genoa against the police were crushed brutally, and by the time the 'war on terror' was underway the forces of the state had effectively outmanoeuvred the movement, galvanised as it was by a seemingly more culturally monolithic enemy.[177] Instead, the complexity and flamboyance of Deleuze & Guattari's prose, combined with their eagerness to be utilised led to the dissemination of their ideas to the point of near-irrelevance; indeed, even by the time they published *What is Philosophy?* in 1991, their disillusionment was tangible:

> Finally, the most shameful moment came when computer science, marketing, design, and advertising, all the disciplines of communication, seized hold of the word concept itself and said: "This is our concern, we are the creative ones, we are the ideas men! We are the friends of the concept, we put it in our computers" [...] The only events are exhibitions, and the only concepts are products that can be sold. Philosophy has not remained unaffected by the general movement that replaced Critique with sales promotion.[178]

This sense that the relentless positivity of the Deleuzo-Guattarian project backfired is exemplified by Slavoj Žižek's anecdote about a globe-trotting yuppie recognising themselves in the language of nomadism and flows that was set in opposition to the very class-interests that they represent. Žižek suggests that Deleuze & Guattari's theoretical edifice was inherently vulnerable to being recaptured when he writes 'There are, effectively, features that justify calling Deleuze the ideologist of late capitalism'.[179] This easy reconstitution is made even more explicit in Eyal Weizman's *Hollow Land*, with its blistering study of how the Israeli Defence Force's attraction to Deleuzian theory manifested itself in concepts such as 'smooth space', used by some among the IDF to describe their practice of blowing holes in the walls of houses in order to facilitate unpredictable movement through the Palestinian refugee camps.[180] This is about as extreme a condition of misuse as can be imagined, but a similar making-aesthetic of an ethical and political system of thought can be found in architecture all throughout the last twenty years. One only has to look at the short-lived fashion for 'folded' buildings around the start of the millennium, as the Deleuzian 'fold' became nothing more than the twisting of the floor at one end of the building to make it appear to be turning into the wall, to see how vacuous the influence could become; indeed, one can argue that the influence of Deleuze has been 'abstract' in the old fashioned way; a series of attractive terms that are inspiring, *regardless* of what their functional context is:

> The concepts of Deleuze meshed well with an emerging digital idiom [...] making deeper interpenetrations of this strain of poststructuralist thought unnecessary [...] the "second [post- Eisenman] generation" saw Deleuzian thought as a natural, more optimistic conceptual foundation for the evolution of experimental architecture, while the "third [parametric] generation" viewed Deleuze's landscape of metaphors far more literally, knowing they could build the kind of catchphrase terms listed above in new and elegant ways using advanced software. This has played out as a relatively a-critical cavalcade of folds and rhizomes, both smooth and striated, over the past 15 years or so.[181]

But even those who are skilled and thorough readers of Deleuze, such as Manuel DeLanda, often have a tendency to exorcise both the Marxist and Freudian ghosts from their systems, in favour of treating Deleuze as a (comparatively) simple materialist-of-flux.[182] But surely even the simplest of class analyses can discern that the use of theoretical language in this way is at least partially a method of separation; a fashionable secret code, the more controversial aspects dropped away to prevent it from causing any irritation to what is still a remarkably bourgeois culture of architects. Furthermore, as we have seen, by shrouding one's practice in the most contemporary language possible, one forecloses certain comparisons and analogies which perhaps would be less than flattering –the 'emperor's new clothes' problem. If that seems too cynical, then perhaps we really ought to ascertain whether or not the digital revolution in architecture has *created any new space.*

It is safe to say that the experimental period of the digital revolution is over, and that we are in a period of consolidation. The 'heretical' experiments of Eisenman et al in the 1990s were set in deliberate opposition to other strands of architecture such as conservative quasi-vernacular, the corporate high tech modernism of Norman Foster or even a revived minimalism; they were mostly unbuilt, with notable but crude exceptions.[183] Now, no such antagonistic positioning exists; approaches to digital design are now preoccupied with new technologies, new methods of fabrication and construction.

One approach is a new kind of techno-environmentalism; at least partially born of a response to the threat of impending ecological catastrophe. According to this approach, the new high-technology design methods should take material and formal principles from the natural world, often at the molecular level; this is rationalised by viewing design in evolutionary terms and evolution in design terms. On the one hand this is admirable; one thing that is vital if humanity is going to avoid the worst of the impending climate induced horror it is the development of newer, more efficient technologies to make society sustainable, not the regression to pre-industrial technologies that some suggest. But on the other, the valorisation of the supposed beauty of nature is fraught with conceptual danger; nature is both emergent order and violent chaos; in the words of Werner Herzog: 'There is a harmony to nature; it is the harmony of overwhelming and collective murder'.[184] This techno-natural attitude is more likely to use organic language to describe new digital architecture; 'genetic algorithms', 'morphogenetic design', 'emergent complexity', 'self organisation'; these terms abound. It concerns itself with studies of cell structures, plant growth models and the material properties of organic materials, its intentions involve 'embedding into buildings the biochemical processes and functionality of life for the advantage of humans, other species and the environment'.[185] The synthesis of the 'industrial' and the 'natural' is a genuinely desirable condition, but it unfortunately presupposes the answers to questions of design; many of the 'smart materials' and other bio-engineering technologies currently being developed have no formal quality of their own; they are visually indistinguishable from existing materials. As a result the designers of this techno-environmentalism tend to resort to previously established languages of complexity or 'nature' when it comes to actually expressing a form: we have not found new space here.

Another important trend accompanying the digital revolution is in the way it manifests itself in academia. In the early period of digital architecture, the lack of appropriate technology to actually *build* what they were designing meant that for most architects the work was speculative and untested; its power was manifested in theoretical and imaginary terms. The real breakthroughs have come with the development of rapid-manufacturing processes to ease the transition of the digital design into a built object. In another example of the increasing commercialism of the contemporary university, one of the tragic cultural developments of the last decade, digital architects are more and more thoroughly tied to industrial interests; their work increasingly involves research which is both commercially oriented and commercially funded.[186] That this is seen as a positive development, a sign of architects being 'tooled up', of being seen to be 'in touch' again, does not bode well. This commercialised design paradigm is primarily concerned with the creation and resolution of form; although perhaps we should use the term 'geometry', seeing that 'form' has a whiff of the capricious about it. Take the following quote concerning the establishment of a commercial research group;

> We recognised that architecture, and design in the broadest sense, was critically dependent on geometry, but that a complete geometric tradition of the understanding of descriptive and construct geometry was being lost through lack of use in a bland planar and orthogonal minimalism or, indeed, through misuse by being excessively indulged at the "hyper" fringes of design. Against this background, the objective of the SmartGeometry Group was to reassert an understanding of geometry in design as more than an "experiential commodity". Rather than being wilful and arbitrary, even the most complex geometry could provide a formal resolution of competing forces and requirements. It could suggest and resolve both structural efficiency and environmental sensitivity.[187]

What we should understand here is an approach to the digital that merely deepens the potentials of the ordinary paradigm – it is the application of parametric design *qua* tools, used merely to optimise a complex object, making it cheaper and simpler to build complicated shapes – there is nothing inherently wrong with this, but it does suggest that the qualitative shift we are looking for is becoming even more elusive, that the method of *enabling* that we saw in Gehry earlier is perhaps more paradigmatic than that of the Deleuzian 'abstract machines'.

Riverside Museum Glasgow, Zaha Hadid, 2011

There are those who still assert that digital architecture has brought us something new, rather than merely an intensification of the old. Perhaps the best example is Patrik Schumacher, who is perhaps the perfect ideologist of digital architecture, being both a partner at Zaha Hadid Architects and a senior academic at the Architectural Association. He makes the provocative move of declaring a new style for 'avant-garde' practice – 'parametricism':

> It succeeds modernism as a new long wave of systematic innovation. The style finally closes the transitional period of uncertainty that was engendered by the crisis of modernism and that was marked by a series of short lived episodes including Postmodernism, Deconstructivism, and

Minimalism. Parametricism is the great new style after modernism.[188]

You have to admire the chutzpah of someone self-proclaiming such a grand style; not since Le Corbusier has an architect been arrogant in such a way. Schumacher even goes so far as to name 'parametricism' *'Der Neue International Style'* in his German translation; an allusion we should extend; whereas it took the erstwhile fascist Philip Johnson to aestheticise the functionalists, the purveyors of 'parametricism' have saved anybody the bother; they have presented themselves as already ideologically blank. According to Schumacher, 'parametricism' emerges from digital tools but is insufficiently defined by them, rather it 'aims for a maximal emphasis on conspicuous differentiation and the visual amplification of differentiating logics. Aesthetically it is the elegance of ordered complexity and the sense of seamless fluidity, akin to natural systems, that is the hallmark of parametricism'.[189] Again there is the appeal to the 'natural', as if it were self-evident that nature required mimicry. As well as this we have the appeal to complexity that has been the hallmark of digital architecture from its inception; the ability of the tools to generate dazzling complexity is seen as its own end, as if it were somehow necessarily better; Schumacher makes his own appeals to the Deleuzian diagram in this regard.[190] What is most insidious about Schumacher's 'parametricism' however is the point in his argument when he allows it to 'touch down' into the world of representation; when he address the nagging question of *why* such emergent complexity is the appropriate form for today's architecture:

This new demand for diversity and complexity has been engendered by the momentous socio-economic restructuring that has been transforming the metropolitan centres over the last 25 years: post-Fordist network economy, globalisation and the attendant, increased lifestyle diversification.[191]

The first question one might ask here is possibly; 'what *are* the demands of the socio-economic era of post-Fordism that are so seemingly self evident?' But even this question is deep in shadow; we should instead try; 'what does Schumacher mean by *demands?*' Does he mean consumer demand? It certainly does not appear that he means political demands. It seems here that Schumacher is casting himself in role of prophet, but then forgetting to have a message to spread. Is it right that a 'style' articulating the very spirit of an age should be nothing but the uncritical reflection of its most banal forces? Does the highly intelligent theorist of complexity not find consumer taste a little more complex than the unproblematic expression of pure 'demands', or *desires?* What becomes almost laughable is that when Schumacher gives the only specific examples of 'new space' that necessitate his parametric approach, namely 'airports, malls, [&] trade exhibitions', they are uncannily reminiscent of the 19th century typologies we have studied here! In all,'Parametricism' has no critical kinks needing unfolding, no potential sticking points needing smoothing out in order to serve the needs of contemporary clients. It cannot be an avant-garde in any real sense, merely an acquiescent pseudo-radicalism.

Out of academia and in the built world we see a remarkable process occurring; the high-tech architects descended from the 'Zoom' wave, those designers of the ditchwater corporate environment, of glass atria and anodized steel, and the post-decon architects of 'the 'Icon', of sight-bites and ego-monuments, are *converging*. Patrik Schumacher is a partner at Zaha Hadid Architects, leading the field of the parametric architects, but at the same time large corporate architects such as Norman Foster have their own special departments for advanced geometry, and specialist parametric engineering firms are just as likely to be hired by minimalists, solutionists or iconists.[192] In this sense we are seeing that even the minor-shock factor of the rebellious architecture of the 90s is being softened out; indeed; one can find similar complex shapes in the work of Hadid for an art museum, Foster for a 'spaceport', or in the roof of any new shopping mall anywhere in the world.[193] Difference is becoming standardised, the unique is becoming generic.

We have spent a lot of this study considering attitudes towards the engineer; from the glory of the mid 19th century to the '1889 syndrome', from the constructivists to the resurrection of the Victorian genius in the guise of the 'solutionist'. Now we should note that the contemporary architecture that is derived from the engineering legacy of the iron & glass palaces has effectively merged with the architecture descended from the spectacular display culture of the great exhibitions; the different strands of the late twentieth century have merged into a structurally literate yet vacuously formalist architecture. But something strange has occurred in this transition; the attitude to engineering has become something it wasn't before. What we have now is the 'resolved shape' model of design: the architect genius comes up with a form that looks spectacular when mocked up as a computer-rendered image viewed from an impossible location at an impossible angle; something that only a satellite can enjoy – a phenomenon known as 'Google Earth urbanism'.[194] This shape might be an abstract 'back of the napkin' effort by the genius architect, or it might be an utterly banal bit of capitalist symbolism; flower petals, strings of pearls, rolling hills... it will inevitably be 'fluid', or 'dynamic'; even if it will never actually move. Any shape is possible; the technology now exists to make it happen; all it needs is to be passed over to the engineer to use their software to figure out how to make it stand up. What we now have as a paradigm for the relationship of architecture to engineering is a near total disassociation. All in all this is far from constituting a new form of space for the digital era; indeed, I would go so far as to suggest that it has more than a little in common with another period of architectural history – the proliferation of styles and approaches, the disassociation of the formal qualities of the architecture and the structural qualities; these are hallmarks of eclecticism. The confusion of having too many options open the designer, the discredited moral arguments, the agonised freedom; the insider knowledge and academic aesthetic systems; all of these are hallmarks of late Victorian design culture.

Conclusion

Should the comparison between contemporary architectural culture and the late 19th century be taken seriously? Although it has a neatness to it, it is not my intention to posit some kind of perfect cycle of history here; it is enough to point out that the bearers of the avant-garde legacy actually have more in common with the culture against which modernism defined itself than they do with radical modernism itself. But though we might crave a repetition of the modernist event, it would be too simple and naïve to expect there to be some new methodology waiting in the wings of architecture, ready to sweep away the academicism and confusion of the current period, defining new forms of space for new cultural movements. But are there lessons we can draw from this problem?

Against the monumentality and eclecticism of the current period of cultural buildings, we might return to our discussion of digital space and note that the hyper-connectivity of the digital world generates similar reactions to those which the iron & glass revolution inspired; it functions both as a symbol of utopia for radicals, democratic, universal, free, but also as a terrifying symbol of control; trails of information, security networks and so on. Perhaps we should be widening the question, and noting that mass-produced architecture never achieved hegemony; our environment is filled with spaces from various times and with various histories; the city *qua* archive is still strong. Perhaps we can posit a not-too-distant time when digital space makes up a large but not overwhelming part of our experience, adding to, overcoding but not replacing previous forms of space. Rather than the virtual reality of the 1980s, we may enter the period of 'augmented reality'. According to this scheme, attempting to create a monumental architectural style for the digital age is no worse than a simple missing of the point, thinking formally in terms of metaphor and historically in terms of the naive cyclicality that we have just warned against. At the same time this missing of the point also strengthens the thesis that we are living in an eclectic age. Despite spending much of the 20th century beyond denigration, there is an impressive madness to late 19th century design; for example the steroidal *Palais de Justice* (1866-) in Brussels, or the fairy-tale Midland Hotel (1866-) that conceals the St. Pancras railway shed in London are both fascinating, overpowering and faintly ridiculous buildings; we can compare these to the flamboyance of a Gehry or Hadid building and conclude that they are similarly over the top, but perhaps endearingly so. If we are being as generous as we can honestly be, we might say that the digital flamboyance of today's most modern architecture constitutes something like a *jugendstil,* an attempt to understand industrialisation/digitisation through filigree and expressiveness.

But this would be too optimistic. The fact is that the poor architecture that manages to get built is a reflection of our depressing political situation. This is nothing new; but certainly it has been strange to see what has happened to modern architecture under the influence of the politics of the last thirty years. The helpless apathy of populations is reflected in the apathy of the designers who are supposedly working at the cutting edge, and this book is at least partly the result of a conviction that the lack of any genuine radicalism in architecture is a deeply negative trend. Hopefully in this book I have managed to shed light upon the ways in which this lack has come about, and alongside the negative cliché of architects being moral prostitutes who will work for anyone, we have at least noted that there have been periods where architects *were* radical, and not just in a naïvely utopian sense. The fact that we have looked at a number of influential thinkers and practitioners in the field and how they have posed as radicals without any concern at all for institutional critique or ethics is a sad state of affairs, and something that needs to change.

If there is one insight that we have gleaned from this study, it is that there was something *unbearable* about iron & glass. The failures, the fires, the neglect, the decline, we have followed the paths of weakness in these buildings; again and again we have seen how deeply contradictory iron & glass was; how it symbolised utopia but played an instrumental role in placating working class antagonism, how it promised the future but was swiftly hidden in the fog of the past, how it quickly out-performed the demands that could be made upon it. It could be read as a fantasy of a better world, but it was also a phantas-magoria, a false dream woven from phantom commodities passively consumed by the gaze - it signified both the nightmare of history and the struggle to awake from it. Iron & glass may well have inaugurated a new regime of immersive capitalist space, but once inaugurated, capital retreated back behind monumentality and massiveness. As well as this, totalitarianisms both Soviet and Nazi would also turn heavily towards monumen-tality, eclecticism and kitsch. Later on, even those who were most influenced by the legacy of iron & glass would simplify its meaning to the point of insignificance.

We have repeatedly stressed how iron & glass buildings inher-ently rejected many of the very concepts that give architecture its cultural power. In light of the failures and the rejections, it is not too hard to see that the qualities that made iron & glass intol-erable are also the very ones that made it so radical. But at the same time we have also seen that these radical qualities are not those of the utopianism usually associated with architecture; the future that iron & glass promised, indeed *still* promises, was that of rain drumming down on innumerable panes of glass; it was the reverberations of sounds gloomily echoing around a space, it was the dim light falling down from dusty glass, it was a skeleton already overwhelmed by nature even from its birth. Beyond these poetic interpretations; its lightness, transparency and ephemerality set it against conventional architecture; it was a form of building which appeared as a Benjaminian allegory of memory, of objective recollection and its attendant forgetfulness. They were ruins without being ruined, fragments even in their totality. This book has been an attempt to grasp this radical melancholy, to retrieve this vision of a deliriously dreary future, to find in the fragments the grains of something utopian even in its very failure.

Acknowledgements

Thank you to Wilma, Robert & Kathryn Murphy for familial support, to Owen Hatherley, Joel Anderson, Ian Abley & Brad Feuerhelm for image assistance, to Kathryn & Owen for reading and comments, to Tariq Goddard and all at Zer0 books, and to everyone else who helped me in some way.

Notes

1. Kohlmaier, G & von Sartory, B, *Houses of Glass*, Cambridge, Mass.; London: MIT Press, 1986, p.27.

2. Giedion, S, *Building in France, Building in Iron, Building in Ferro-Concrete*, Santa Monica: Getty Centre, 1995, p.111 – 'The common characteristic of these buildings is that they serve transient purposes: market halls, railroad stations, exhibitions'.

3. See for example Fergusson, J, *History of the Modern Styles of Architecture*, London: John Murray, 1891, p.413 'The point, however, at which the engineer and the architect come most directly in contact is in the erection of stations and station buildings. In every instance these ought to be handed over to the architect as soon as the engineer has arranged the mechanical details.'

4. Benjamin, W, *The Arcades Project*, Cambridge, Mass.; London: Belknap Press, 1999, p.14.

5. *Houses of Glass*, p.1 – 'The nineteenth century glasshouse was like a museum in which the masterpieces of nature were gathered together, listed in a catalogue, and preserved for the future.'

6. *Houses of Glass*, p.152.

7. To take just one example; 'The Crystal Palace, as a product of Victorian England, was one of the most influential buildings ever erected. Innovative in structure, completely new in its function, unusual in its form and significant in the associations it embodied, it takes its place with a handful of other pre-eminent buildings such as the Pantheon, Hagia Sophia, and Abbot Sugar's St. Denis' (Kihlstedt, F.T., *The Crystal Palace*, Scientific American, 1984, quoted in Greenhalgh, P. *Ephemeral Vistas: a History of the Expositions Universelles, Great Exhibitions and World's Fairs, 1851-1939*, Manchester: Manchester University Press, 1988,

p.150).

8. The 1798 Industrial Exhibition in Paris is often cited as the very first, but the 'exhibition' at least partly grew from 'fairs' that had been held throughout the previous century.

9. *The Arcades Project*, p.201.

10. Sloterdijk, P, *Im Weltinnenraum des Kapitals*, Frankfurt am Main: Suhrkamp, 2005, p.266 – 'Mit ihm began eine neue Ästhetik der Immersion ihren Siegeszug durch die Moderne.'

11. Speech by Prince Albert at the opening of the Crystal Palace, 1851 quoted in Gillooly, E, 'Rhetorical Remedies for Taxonomic Troubles', in Buzard, J, Childers, J.W. & Gillooly, E (eds.), *Victorian Prism: Refractions of the Crystal Palace*, Charlottesville; London: University of Virginia Press, 2007. p.26.

12. Frampton, K, *Modern Architecture: A Critical History*, London: Thames & Hudson, 2007. p.34.

13. *History of the Modern Styles of Architecture*, p.420.

14. Derrida's work is filled with the figure of the ghost; especially from the end of the 1980s onwards. The most important text in this regard is *Spectres of Marx*, New York; London: Routledge, 1994.

15. Armstrong, I, 'Languages of Glass', in *Victorian Prism*, p.58.

16. Speech by Prince Albert, March 1850, quoted in Davis, J.R., 'The Great Exhibition and Modernisation', in *Victorian Prism*, p.235.

17. Buzard, J, 'Conflicting Cartographies', in *Victorian Prism*, p.40.

18. *Ephemeral Vistas*, p.29.

19. 'The Great Exhibition and Modernisation', in *Victorian Prism*, p.235.

20. Auerbach, J, *The Great Exhibition of 1851: A Nation on Display*, New Haven, CT: Yale University Press, 1999, p.193.

21. *The Builder*, 10th May 1852.

22. *Houses of Glass,* p.109.
23. *The Graphic,* 13th June 1885.
24. *Paxton, J,* Speech to Parliament 28th January 1852, quoted in Chadwick, G.F, *The Works of Joseph Paxton,* Architectural P, 1961, p.143.
25. Figures from *The Works of Joseph Paxton,* appendix.
26. *History of the Modern Styles of Architecture,* p.420 It should be noted that Fergusson himself would be involved in the art direction of the interior of the Sydenham Palace. This did not stop him from suggesting that the Sydenham Palace required a more massive, more monumental masonry aspect to it to raise it to the level of 'great' architecture, however.
27. The Crystal Palace, Sydenham. To be sold by auction on Tuesday 28th day of November, 1911, *London : Hudson & Kearns, 1911. p.11.*
28. *The Crystal Palace Company. Deed of Settlement, Royal Charters and List of Shareholders,* London: H.G. Bohn, 1856, p.5 – 'Object and business of the company: That the objects and business of the said company shall be the purchasing of the great exhibition building in Hyde Park, [...] the forming and maintaining Conservatories, Parks and Museums in conjunction with the said building for the illustration and advancement of the Arts, Sciences and Manufactures, and the cultivation of a refined taste amongst all classes of the community.'
29. Phillips, S, *Official General Guide to the Crystal Palace and Park, Sydenham,* Robert K. Burt, Crystal Palace Printing Office, 1862. p.131.
30. See: Venturi, R, Scott-Brown, D & Izenour, S, *Learning from Las Vegas,* London: M.I.T. Press, 1972. Simply put; the 'decorated shed' is a rudimentary structure where the meaning is expressed through ornament, whereas the 'duck' is a building which communicates wholly through its

structure.

31. See the *Official General Guide to the Crystal Palace and Park* for a complete list.

32. Perhaps the closest analogies would be the Pergamon Museum in Berlin (1910-) in which entire buildings were transported and re-erected within the new building, sometimes becoming part of a hybrid edifice, or the Cast Court of the V&A museum (1899-), in which full scale fragmented replicas of significant architectural details are stored. Both of these spaces are remarkable, but neither of these two conditions are quite as intense as the courts of the Sydenham Palace appear to have been.

33. Derrida, J, 'Freud and the Scene of Writing', in *Writing and Difference*, London: Routledge, 2001, pp.246-91. This essay is an examination of Freud's use of a writing metaphor to describe the process of memory accumulation.

34. Eastlake, E, 'The Crystal Palace', in *Quarterly Review 96*, March 1855, quoted in Gurney, P, 'A Palace for the People' in *Victorian Prism*, pp.138-41.

35. Flint, K, 'Exhibiting America', in *Victorian Prism*, p.171.

36. For a discussion of the contradictory Victorian attitudes to the nudity of the Greek Slave and other sculptures, see Teukolsky, R, 'This Sublime Museum', in *Victorian Prism*, pp.89-93.

37. Piggot, J, *Palace of the People: The Crystal Palace at Sydenham 1854-1936*. London: C. Hurst, 2004. p.52.

38. Benjamin, W, *The Origin of German Tragic Drama*, London: Verso, 1998, p.178.

39. *The Arcades Project*, p.328 – 'The allegories stand for that which the commodity makes of the experiences people have in this century.' We will have occasion to come back to this notion when we compare allegory to spectrality.

40. *The Arcades Project*, p.300.

41. *The Origin of German Tragic Drama*, p.177.

42. See Musgrave, M, *The Musical Life of the Crystal Palace*, Cambridge: Cambridge University Press, 1995.

43. The Musical Life of the Crystal Palace, p.42.

    There are numerous examples of contemporary accounts of the acoustic properties of the Crystal Palaces; Musgrave quotes the *Musical Times* referring to the 'fogginess and uncertainty' of the sound of the concerts. In fact one can approximately experience this in the acoustic qualities of the railway sheds, which reverberate and muffle sound as if one were underwater.

44. This is true to a certain extent; the phonautogram, which was developed by Édouard-Léon Scott de Martinville, certainly existed before the phonograph (the earliest recording is from 1860), although with this method (which actually utilised the engraving of a sound wave into ash!) there was no way to replay the sound. Recently however, new digital techniques have led to vague recreations of the original sound. As well as this, the Edison company made a number of failed attempts to record music before the event described above. See *http://www.firstsounds.org/* (accessed 18-04-2010).

45. For digital recordings of the earliest Edison recordings, see the Edison National Historic Site, where one can listen to the 1888 Crystal Palace recording. *http://www.nps.gov/archive/edis/edisonia/very_early.htm* (accessed 18-04-2010).

46. Jameson, F, 'Marx's Purloined Letter', in Sprinker, M, (ed.), *Ghostly Demarcations: A Symposium on Jacques Derrida's Spectres of Marx*, London: Verso, 1999, p.64.

47. Allwood, J, *The Great Exhibitions*, London: Studio Vista, 1977. p.41.

48. Gurney, P, 'A Palace for the People?', in *Victorian Prism*, p.147.

49. Anonymous ('The Shorthand Writer'), *The Crystal Palace in*

Adversity; the Duty of Raising it to National Usefulness, with Special Reminiscences of the Great Exhibition of 1851, London: 1876, p.11; p.19.

50. Bell Knight, C-F, *The Rise and Fall of the Biggest Ever Glass Container*, Bath: 1977. p.49.

51. See Allwood, J, *The Great Exhibitions*, London: Vista, 1977.

52. See *Houses of Glass* for a near-complete taxonomic list of iron & glass buildings.

53. Ensing, R, 'The Albert Palace Battersea', in *The Wandsworth Historian*, 1985 vol. 45 p.1.

54. *The Builder*, March 1st 1884, pp.316-7.

55. *The Civil Engineer and Architect's Journal*, April 1st 1866.

56. *The Builder*, May 2nd 1885, p.634.

57. *Houses of Glass*, p.110.

58. *The Builder*, May 2nd 1885, p.634.

59. *Albert Palace Picture Gallery, Descriptive Catalogue*, London: Dunn, Collin & Co. 1885.

60. *Plan of the Albert Palace, Battersea Park. For Sale*, London: 1888.

61. *The Builder*, March 1st 1884, pp.316-7.

62. *The Builder*, May 2nd 1885, p.634.

63. *The Musical World*, June 13th 1885, p.365.

64. *The Builder*, June 13th 1885, p.852.

65. Indeed; it also rained at the opening of the Great Exhibition. See Allwood, J *The Great Exhibitions*, London: Studio Vista, p.20. Allwood quotes Queen Victoria's diary; 'A little rain fell, just as we started, but before we neared the Crystal Palace, the sun shone and gleamed upon the gigantic edifice, upon which the flags of every nation were flying'.

66. *The South-Western Star*, November 5th 1892.

67. Posters from the *Evanion Collection*, British Library. Evan.265, 1885; Evan.2538, 1886; Evan.1161, 1881 respectively.

68. *The Builder*, August 19th 1893, p.134.

69   *The South-Western Star,* April 30th 1892.

70.   *The South-Western Star,* May 14th 1892.

71.   *The South-Western Star,* October 15th 1892 (Walter Besant was a Victorian novelist who established the 'People's Palace' in East London; another long lost iron & glass palace).

72.   *The South-Western Star,* October 15th 1892.

73.   *The South-Western Star,* October 22nd, 1892
Passmore Edwards' autobiography makes no mention whatsoever of the Albert Palace. See Passmore Edwards, J, *A Few Footprints,* London: Watts & Co., 1906. It is also notable that Passmore Edwards' philanthropic building spree only began in 1892; the Albert Palace would have been one of the very first of his efforts. See Best, R.S, *The Life and Good Works of John Passmore Edwards,* Redruth: Truran Publications, 1981.

74   *The South-Western Star,* January 13th, 1894 / *Hansard, Jan 8th 1894,* HC Deb 08 January 1894 vol 20 c1024, *http://hansard.millbanksystems.com/commons/1894/jan/08/alber t-palace-battersea* (accessed 18-04-2010).

75.   *The South-Western Star,* June 2nd 1894.

76.   The property developers ignored my request for information.

77.   'The Kensington Canal, railways and related developments', *Survey of London: volume 42: Kensington Square to Earl's Court* (1986), pp. 322-338. *http://www.british-history.ac.uk/report.aspx?compid=50329&strquery=Albert Palace* (accessed 18-04-2010).

78.   *The South-Western Star,* May 14th 1892 (the Alexandra Palace is actually still extant, although it is under constant threat of being redeveloped).

79.   Regarding the problem of water ingress and iron & glass; 'Only a year after the Palace opened, Paxton was told at a meeting that rain poured 'in torrents' through the roof

among the exhibitors, and replied that it was 'as good as any railway station roof'.' *The Observer*, 15th July 1855, quoted in Piggott, J, *Palace of the People,* London: C. Hurst, 2004, p.44.

80. Benjamin, W, *The Arcades Project,* p.24.

81. Derrida, J, *Archive Fever,* Chicago: University of Chicago Press, 1996, p.84.

82. Benjamin, W. 'Experience and Poverty', in *Selected Writings, Vol.2,* Cambridge, Mass.: Belknap Press, 1996, pp.733-4.

83. See Chadwick, *The Works of Joseph Paxton.*

84. *Houses of Glass,* p.320.

85. *Houses of Glass,* p.2.

86. Howard, E, *Garden Cities of Tomorrow,* London: Swan Sonnenschein & co. 1902.

87. Chernyshevsky, N.G, *What is to be Done?* London: Virago, 1982, p.323.

88. Dostoyevsky, F, *Notes from the Underground,* Oxford: Oxford University Press, 1991. See part I, chapters 8-10.

89. Berman, M, *All That Is Solid Melts Into Air,* New York: Simon and Schuster, 1982, p.238.

90. Fergusson, J, *History of the Modern Styles of Architecture,* p.420.

91. Hitchcock, H R & Johnson, P, *The International Style,* New York: Museum of Modern Art, 1932.

92. Hitchcock, H.R, *Modern Architecture in England,* New York: Museum of Modern Art, 1937, p.10.

93. *Modern Architecture in England,* p.12.

94. Giedion, S, *Building in France, Building in Iron, Building in Ferro-Concrete,* Santa Monica: Getty Centre, 1995 p.85.

95. *Building in France...* p.86.

96. *Building in France...* p.122 and p. 124 respectively.

97. Giedion, S, *Space, Time and Architecture,* Cambridge, Mass. London: Harvard University Press, 1967, p.252.

98. *Building in France...* p.135.

99. See McKean, J; Durant, S & Parissien, S, *Lost Masterpieces,*

London: Phaidon, 2000.

100. BBC interview with Nicholas Grimshaw, http://www.bbc. co.uk/radio3/johntusainterview/grimshaw_transcript.shtml (accessed 19-04-2010).

101. Although impressionist painters would be attracted to them; see Pisarro's painting of the Crystal Palace, or Monet's paintings of train stations.

102. Le Corbusier, 'The Crystal Palace : a Tribute', in Murray, I & Osley, J. (eds.), *Le Corbusier and Britain*, Abingdon: Routledge, 2009, pp.106-8.

103. Frampton, K, 'Industrialisation and the Crises in Architecture', in Michael Hays. K (ed.), *Oppositions Reader*, New York: Princeton Architectural Press, 1998, p.47.

104. Quoted in Lynton, N, *Tatlin's Tower: Monument to Revolution*, New Haven, Conn. London: Yale University Press, 2009, p.103.

105. Dillon, B, 'Poetry of Metal', in *The Guardian*, 25th July 2009, http://www.guardian.co.uk/books/2009/jul/25/vladimir-tatlins-tower-st-petersburg?FORM=ZZNR7 (accessed 26-4-2010).

106. See the film made by MIT's Takehiko Nagakura as part of the series *Unbuilt Monuments* (1999).

107. Dillon, B, 'Poetry of Metal'.

108. http://news.bbc.co.uk/1/hi/entertainment/2509465.stm (accessed 19-04-2010).

109. Fuller, R. Buckminster, *Ideas & Integrities*, Toronto: Macmillan, 1969, p.12.

110. *Ideas & Integrities*, p.54.

111. Piggott, J, *Palace of the People*, London: C. Hurst, 2004, p.180 & p.211.

112. Conekin, B, *The Autobiography of a Nation: The 1951 Festival of Britain*, Manchester: Manchester University Press, 2003, p.229.

113. Banham, R, 'The Style: 'Flimsy...Effeminate'?', in Banham,

M. & Hillier, B. (eds.), *A Tonic to the Nation : The Festival of Britain 1951*, London: Thames and Hudson, 1976, p.197.

114. Cook, P, *Experimental Architecture*, London: Studio Vista, 1970, p.22.

115. Sadler, S, *Archigram – Architecture without Architecture*, London: MIT press, 2005, p.103.

116. *Experimental Architecture*, p.12.

117. *Archigram – Architecture without Architecture*, p.166.

118. Baudrillard, J. & Nouvel, J, *The Singular Objects of Architecture*, Minneapolis: University of Minnesota Press, 2002, p.38.
   The centre sits on the Rue Beaubourg, a title that many give to the building rather than calling it after Pompidou.

119. Colquhoun, A, 'Plateau Beaubourg', in *Essays in Architectural Criticism: Modern Architecture and Historical Change*, London: MIT Press, 1981, p.117 – 'It is difficult to envisage any function which would require an unimpeded fifty-meter span with a height limitation of seven meters'.

120. *Plateau Beaubourg*, p.114.

121. Indeed; there exists a direct pastiche of the Crystal Palace: the Infomart Building (1985-) in Dallas.

122. Quoted in : Fraser, M & Kerr, J, *Architecture and the Special Relationship*, London: Routledge, 2007, p.304.

123. BBC interview with Nick Grimshaw, *http://www.bbc.co.uk/radio3/johntusainterview/grimshaw_transcript.shtml* (last accessed 31-03-2010).

124. Barker, P, 'A Womb Without a View', *New Statesman*, 13-12-1999.

125. Benjamin, W, *The Arcades Project*, p.150.

126 Giedion, S, *Building in France, Building in Iron, Building in Ferroconcrete*, Santa Monica: The Getty Centre, 1995, p.117.

127. *Archigram – Architecture without Architecture*, p.134.

128. *Architecture and the Special Relationship*, p.306.

129. See Jencks, C, *The Language of Post-Modern Architecture*,

London: Academy Editions, 1977.

130. Brolin, B, *The Failure of Modern Architecture*, New York: Van Nostrand Reinhold Co., 1976, p.8.

131. See Venturi, R, Scott-Brown, D & Izenour, S, *Learning from Las Vegas*, London: M.I.T. Press, 1972.

132. In Archigram's case it was the Architectural Association school in the UK.

133. See: Sokal, D & Bricmont, J, *Intellectual Impostures : Postmodern Philosophers' Abuse of Science*, London: Profile, 1998. This infamous book was born after Alan Sokal, a physicist, successfully submitted a hoax article consisting of 'nonsense' to a social-theory journal.

134. For example, take the attempt by a number of academics to deny Derrida the honorary degree he had been awarded from Cambridge University in 1992, claiming that 'M. Derrida's work does not meet accepted standards of clarity and rigour'

135. See Eisenman, P, 'Post-Functionalism', in Hays, K. Michael (ed.), *Oppositions Reader: Selected Readings from a Journal for Ideas and Criticism in Architetcure 1973-1984*, New York: Princeton Architectural Press, 1998, p.11.

136 'Post-Functionalism', p.10.

137. Eisenman, P, *Diagram Diaries*, London: Thames & Hudson, 1999, p.92.

138. Just one example: 'While all discourses, Derrida would argue, contain repressions that in turn contain an alternative interior representation, architecture must be seen as a special case because of its privileging of presence. If Derrida is correct, there is already given in the interiority of architecture a form of representation, perhaps as the becoming unmotivated of the architectural sign. This repressed form of representation is not only interior to architecture, but anterior to it. It is this representation in architecture that could also be called a writing. How this

writing enters into the diagram becomes a critical issue for architecture.' *Diagram Diaries*, p.32

139. Kipnis, J, 'Introduction', in Eisenman, P, *Written into the Void: Selected Writings, 1990-2004*, New Haven, Conn.: Yale University Press, 2007, p.xxvii.

140. Derrida, J, and Eisenman, P, *Chora L Works*, New York: Monacelli Press, 1997. It should be noted that Eisenman shows good humour in publishing something in which he comes across rather badly.

141. *Chora L Works*, p.9.

142. *Chora L Works*, p.105.

143. Benjamin, W, 'Experience and Poverty', in *Selected Writings Vol.2*, Cambridge, Mass.: Belknap Press / Harvard University Press, 1996, p.733.

144. Eisenman, P, *Diagram Diaries*, pp.194-7. Eisenman uses the metaphor of walking on a beach; the foot leaves an imprint in the sand, but the beach leaves a trace of sand upon the foot.

145. 'Experience and Poverty', p.734'

146. Derrida, J, 'Letter to Peter Eisenman', in *Written into the Void*, p.165 (this is the same letter from the end of *Chora L Works*, however in a better translation and without the holes cut into the middle of the paper).

147. 'Letter to Peter Eisenman', p.165.

148. Derrida, J, *Archive Fever*, Chicago, London: University of Chicago Press, 1996, p.84.

149. *Chora L Works*, p.188.

150. Johnson, P. and Wigley, M, *Deconstructivist Architecture*, New York :Museum of Modern Art, 1988. p.7.

151. *Deconstructivist Architecture*, p.16.

152. *Deconstructivist Architecture*, p.17.

153. All of these words come from Wigley's introduction to *Deconstructivist Architecture*, pp.10-17.

154. Cooke, C, 'Images or Intelligence?', in *Russian Constructivism*

& *Iakov Chernikhov, Architectural Design*, Vol.59 No 7/8, London, 1988, p.VII.

155. Although admittedly this is not really so different to Le Corbusier, who continued to paint nearly every day of his working life.

156. Meades, J *On the Brandwagon*, BBC, 2007.

157. Indeed, Gehry himself would later describe the notion of the 'Bilbao Effect', a single building effecting economic change as 'Bullshit'. *The Times Online*, July 9th 2008, *http://entertainment.timesonline.co.uk/tol/arts_and_entertainment/visual_arts/architecture_and_design/article4304855.ec e* (accessed 9-4-2010).

158. Zaha Hadid Architects, *Cairo Expo City*, 2009, http://www.dezeen.com/2009/06/09/cairo-expo-city-by-zaha-hadid-architects/ (accessed 26-04-2010).

159. Zaha Hadid Architects, *Regium Waterfront*, 2009, http://www.dezeen.com/2009/02/09/regium-waterfront-by-zaha-hadid-architects/ (accessed 26-04-2010).

160. Zaha Hadid Architects, *The Stone Towers*, 2009, http://www.dezeen.com/2009/05/28/the-stone-towers-by-zaha-hadid-architects/ (accessed 26-04-2010).

161. Zaha Hadid Architects, *Jesolo Magica – Retail & Business Centre*, 2010. http://www.dezeen.com/2010/03/11/jesolo-magica-by-zaha-hadid-architects/ (accessed 26-04-2010).

162. The term 'yuppiedrome' was coined by the artist Laura Oldfield Ford.

163. Colquhoun, A, 'Plateau Beaubourg', in *Essays in Architectural Criticism: Modern Architecture and Historical Change*, London: MIT Press, 1981, p.112.

164. *On the Brandwagon.*

165. Benjamin, W, *The Arcades Project*, pp.150-5.

166. For example; Birkhauser's series of books on the 'IT Revolution in Architecture' would focus on only three individual firms; Hadid, Gehry and Eisenman.

167. For a Derridean discussion of email; see *Archive Fever* pp.15-18.
For Derrida's inclusion of commodity relations within his system, see *Spectres of Marx*.

168. Deleuze, G, *The Fold: Leibniz and the Baroque*, London: Athlone Press, 1993.

169. Eisenman, P, 'Folding in Time: The Singularity of Rebstock', in *Blurred Zones: Investigations of the Interstitial: Eisenman Architects 1988-1998*, New York: Monacelli Press, 2003, p.131.

170. 'Folding in Time', p. 132.

171. Deleuze, G, & Guattari, F, *A Thousand Plateaux: Capitalism & Schizophrenia, translated by Brian Massumi*, London: Continuum, 2004, p.157.

172. It would be a mistake here to understand the word 'Idea' here in the Platonic sense; Deleuze expends a lot of effort distinguishing the concepts. For example: 'The nature of the Idea is to be distinct and obscure. In other words, the Idea is precisely *real without being actual, differentiated without being differenciated, and complete without being entire* (Deleuze, G, *Difference and Repetition*, London: Athlone Press, 1994, p.266).

173. *Difference and Repetition*, p.260.

174. Deleuze is careful to remind his reader of this, although one might reasonably ask why the following kind of disclaimer would be necessary at all: 'at this point the philosophy of difference must be wary of turning into the discourse of beautiful souls: differences, nothing but differences, in a peaceful coexistence in the Idea of social places and functions ... but the name of Marx is sufficient to save it from this danger' (*Difference and Repetition*, p.259).

175. Software commonly in use in 2010 includes 'embedded' programming languages such as MAXscript (for 3DSMax) and MEL (for Maya), found in programmes used primarily for the animation industry, or more intuitive systems such as

Grasshopper (for Rhino) and Generative Components (for Microstation).

176. DeLanda, M, 'Deleuze and the Use of the Genetic Algorithm in Architecture', http://www.cddc.vt.edu/host/delanda/pages/algorithm.html (accessed 11-4-2010).

177. Note how the use of new 'anti-terror' legislation has been frequently utilised to effectively stifle anti-capitalist protest in the years since 2001.

178. Deleuze, G & Guattari, F, *What is Philosophy?* New York: Columbia University Press, 1994, p.10.

179. Žižek, S, *Organs without Bodies,* London: Routledge, 2004, pp.183-4.

180. Weizman, E, *Hollow Land,* London: Verso, 2007.

181. Payne, J, 'A Conversation between Sanford Kwinter and Jason Payne', in Sakamoto, T & Ferré, A. (eds.), *From Control to Design: Parametric/Algorithmic Architecture,* New York: Actar-D, 2008, p.226.

182. See DeLanda, M, *Intensive Science and Virtual Philosophy,* London: Continuum, 2002; or *A New Philosophy of Society,* London: Continuum, 2006. DeLanda's drastically reduced assemblage theory has been influential upon a large number of architects; indeed, his writings are often cited as introductory texts for Deleuze

183. See for example; Greg Lynn's Presbyterian Church (1998), or Lars Spuybroek's Son-O-House (2004).

184. Quoted from Blank, L, dir. *Burden of Dreams,* 1982.

185. Hensel, M, 'Towards Self-Organisational and Multiple-Performance Capacity in Architecture', in *Techniques and Technologies in Morphogenetic Design, Architectural Design, Vol.76, No.2,* London: Wiley Academy, 2006, p.25.

186. See Stefan Collini's article on the Research Excellence Framework, *Times Literary Supplement,* 13-11-2009.

187. Hesselgren, L, quoted in Menges, A, 'Instrumental

Geometry', in *Techniques and Technologies in Morphogenetic design*, p.43.

188. Schumacher, P, 'Parametricism – A New Global Style for Architecture and Urban Design', originally published in *Digital Cities, Architectural Design, Vol.79, No.4*, http://www.patrikschumacher.com/Texts/Parametricism%20 %20A%20New%20Global%20Style%20for%20Architecture %20and%20Urban%20Design.html (accessed 15-4-2010).

189. Schumacher, P, 'Parametricism'.

190. Schumacher, P, 'Parametric Diagrammes', originally published in *The Diagrams of Architecture*, London: Wiley, 2010.http://www.patrikschumacher.com/Texts/Parametric% 20Diagrammes.html accessed 15-04-2010.

191. Schumacher, P, *The Autopoiesis of Architecture*, London: Wiley, 2011, p.292

192. Swiss firm Design to Production have worked on projects for minimalists SANAA, post-high tech solutionists Renzo Piano, and iconists Zaha Hadid.

193. The firm 'MAKE', headed by ex-Fosters partner Ken Shuttleworth is particularly terrible in this regard; purveying a kind of frivolous corporate shapery that is just awful.

194. I am indebted to architect Finn Williams, from whom I first heard this term.

Contemporary culture has eliminated both the concept of the public and the figure of the intellectual. Former public spaces – both physical and cultural – are now either derelict or colonized by advertising. A cretinous anti-intellectualism presides, cheerled by expensively educated hacks in the pay of multinational corporations who reassure their bored readers that there is no need to rouse themselves from their interpassive stupor. The informal censorship internalized and propagated by the cultural workers of late capitalism generates a banal conformity that the propaganda chiefs of Stalinism could only ever have dreamt of imposing. Zer0 Books knows that another kind of discourse – intellectual without being academic, popular without being populist – is not only possible: it is already flourishing, in the regions beyond the striplit malls of so-called mass media and the neurotically bureaucratic halls of the academy. Zer0 is committed to the idea of publishing as a making public of the intellectual. It is convinced that in the unthinking, blandly consensual culture in which we live, critical and engaged theoretical reflection is more important than ever before.